I0828528

Bateleur Pair

Juvenile Gabar Goshawk

KGALAGADI SELF-DRIVE BIRDS

Text by **Philip & Ingrid van den Berg**

Photos by **Philip & Ingrid van den Berg**
Heinrich van den Berg

Published by **HPH Publishing**

van den berg

Bateleur with Nesting Material

Contents

Kgalagadi Scene

The Kgalagadi Transfrontier Park spells paradise to some, but is not a place for the faint-hearted visitor. While it is a place with extra-large blue skies, sun-baked red dunes, pale green three-thorn bushes, silky bushman's grasses dancing in the wind and dry riverbeds fringed by camelthorns, it is uncomfortably hot with sand and dust that penetrates everything, extra-bright sunlight that blinds one's vision, almost non-existent shade and dust storms that darken the skies.

But beware, once you get used to it, you will be hooked for life.

Polentswa Waterhole

Common Ostrich Dust-bathing

INTRODUCTION

The semi-arid Kgalagadi Transfrontier Park is situated in the remote northern part of the Northern Cape Province of South Africa and the southwestern tip of Botswana. It comprises about eight percent of the largest single expanse of sand on Earth, the great Kalahari Basin, and is dominated by two dry (fossil) river courses: the Auob and the Nossob. While most of the park is covered by typical semi-arid savanna, in the southwest, this gives way to a huge region of long parallel rows of sparsely vegetated bright-red sinuous dunes rising to 15 metres above the valleys or dune streets. It makes the Kgalagadi Transfrontier Park stunningly different from any other game reserve in Africa.

The 3.7 million hectare park is unique in many ways, not least in that it straddles two countries and is one of only a few conservation areas of this magnitude left in the world. It is an amalgamation of the 0.9 million hectares of South Africa's former Kalahari Gemsbok National Park and the 2.8 million hectares of Botswana's Gemsbok National Park, which are now managed as a unit. This makes sense since there has never been a fence between the two countries and animals have always been able to cross the border without passport formalities.

The two fossil rivers, the Nossob and the Auob, are mostly dry and are the main features of the park. They have their origins in Namibia where the inconsistent rains seldom deliver enough water to cause flow through the park. Their beds are lined with deep-rooted trees, reaching the ancient water table beneath. Several boreholes in the riverbeds supply drinking water for the animals and are lifelines in times of drought.

MAP OF KGALAGADI TRANSFRONTIER PARK

The Kalahari is a vibrant semi-desert, with a surprising abundance of life and a big sky, displaying spectacular sunrises, sunsets, thunderstorms and glittering starry nights. The vast open spaces, covered in rich earthy colours, and with a remarkable abundance of desert-adapted animals and plants, make this place of contrasts addictive.

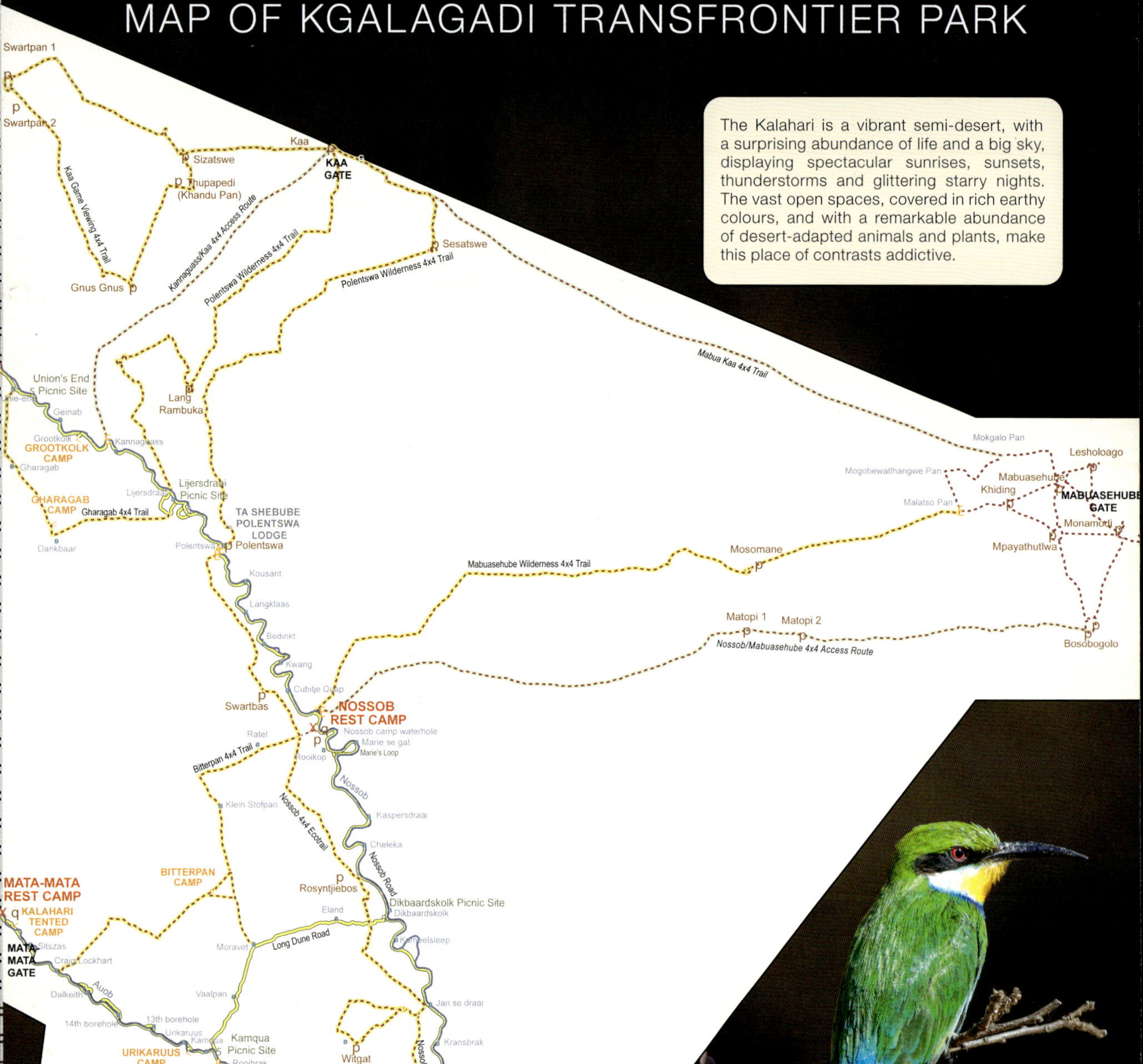

Swallow-tailed Bee-eater

Black-chested Snake Eagle

MAKING THE MOST OF THIS BOOK

The Kgalagadi Transfrontier Park, with its arid savanna environment, provides a unique and exciting backdrop for honing bird identification skills. Its biodiversity, though less expansive than that of lusher regions, offers a distinctive opportunity for focused learning. Many first-time visitors to the Kgalagadi – initially indifferent to birding – are often captivated by the abundance of raptors, vibrant avifauna and diverse birdlife. The park's modest species count makes it an accessible entry point for newcomers venturing into the world of birds.

While numerous comprehensive bird reference books are available for southern Africa, distinguishing between closely related species – some not found in the park – can pose significant challenges. That is where this book becomes extremely useful. It focuses on the 179 recorded resident species, providing practical and applicable knowledge for bird identification in the Kgalagadi Transfrontier Park.

This guide will help you identify the bird species most commonly seen in the park. It also delves into bird behaviour's intricacies and adaptations to the challenging semi-arid environment.

Rather than overwhelming readers with exhaustive information on every bird species they might encounter, they focus on those frequently sighted birds exhibiting notable behavioural and structural adaptations. **Text boxes** describe the critical characteristics of the various **bird families** into which species are grouped. Understanding the traits of each family enhances individual identification. Additionally, the book categorises the number of regularly present species within each family as **true residents**, **annual migrants** or **nomads** (birds that move from place to place without regard to direction or season). Over 160 **vagrants** or incidental visitors have been recorded but are not regarded as residents or discussed in this book.

We designated certain species as '**star species**'. For some of these, we depicted their appearance and enriched the descriptions with insight into their lifestyles and survival strategies in the extreme environmental conditions of the Kalahari.

The selection of photographs in this book aims to **facilitate identification** while showcasing the beauty and diversity of each bird. It's unlikely visitors will encounter all mentioned species in a single park visit. However, this serves as an incentive to explore the park across various seasons over many years. Most birds congregate in the tree-lined dry riverbeds, while others inhabit the dunes and are often spotted when driving along the dune roads or 4x4 trails. Rest camps provide refuge for several species. Look out for nesting birds and roosting owls. Viewing hides at the waterholes offer good birding.

The layout of the book

There are two chapters. The first serves as background reading for the second chapter, which deals with knowledge that will enhance your birding experience.

We have arranged the different bird families and species **according to their feeding habits and habitat preferences**. We start the second chapter with raptors or carnivorous birds; then move on to terrestrial birds with long legs; birds that hunt insects in flight; smaller birds that hunt from a perch; smaller birds foraging in and around trees and shrubs; omnivorous birds; fruit-eating and nectar-feeding birds; smaller terrestrial birds in open areas; seedeaters with soft bills; and birds feeding in and around water.

Tips for identifying birds

If you want to enjoy watching birds, a good pair of binoculars is necessary. Focusing on their most prominent characteristics is helpful when identifying birds, as it encompasses factors such as **size** and **plumage coloration**. Pay attention to **distinctive bands of colour** on the breast and head, as well as the **colour of the bill and eyes**. Remain observant for **markings on the rump** or **bands on the tail**, which may become apparent when the bird is in flight.

Northern Black Korhaan

Scientific nomenclature

While scientific names may appear irrelevant to beginners, they serve an important purpose. Scientific names remain consistent worldwide, unlike common names, which can vary between countries for some bird species.

Within each **family**, birds are classified by **genus** and **species**. Most family groups can be further divided into **sub-families**, but we refer to sub-families only in a few cases where it makes sense. Birds within the **same genus** are usually **closely related and share behavioural and appearance similarities**, while **members of the same species** are even more closely related and **can interbreed**. Both generic and species names are **italicised**, with the **generic name capitalised** and the **species name in lowercase**.

Example

Look at the common and scientific name of the **Yellow-billed Kite (*Milvus aegyptius*)**. All three kites in the Kgalagadi have 'kite' in their common name: Black-winged Kite, Yellow-billed Kite, and Black Kite. However, examining their scientific names reveals distinctions. The Yellow-billed Kite (*Milvus aegyptius*) and the Black Kite (*Milvus migrans*) belong to the same genus, whereas the Black-winged Kite (*Elanus caeruleus*) does not.

Happy birding!

A PLACE OF EXTREMES

The Kgalagadi is a place of extremes. Temperature fluctuations are considerable and in the winter months it can range from –10°C at night, upwards of 30°C during the day. In summer, the temperature at night can drop to 5°C, but day temperatures can quickly rise to 45°C in the shade. The sand surface can reach up to 70°C, about 20 degrees more than in the shade. Temperatures can vary by up to 30°C or more in a single day.

A sand mantle covers most of the park and the different types of landscape or ecozones are subtle. Sands of the Kgalagadi have a high iron content, and they weather to a bright orange-red, giving the region its characteristic background colour. It is partly because of the sandy nature of the soil that this region lacks surface water. The average annual rainfall ranges from 150 mm in the southwest to 450 mm in the northeast in Botswana and occurs mainly in summer. Most of the showers are localised and vicious thunderstorms are of short duration. The water drains into the sand and is usually insufficient to sustain the flowing river, which one would expect a river to do.

The two fossil rivers in the park are bone dry. The Nossob River flows on average only once every 100 years, while the Auob flows for a reasonable distance on average once every 10 or 11 years. However, plenty of underground moisture enables the growth of relatively profuse plant life along these dead rivers. Drilling boreholes for water before the land became a national park has enabled the region to open for stock farming. It has allowed previously migratory or nomadic animals (including many birds) to become residents.

THE ARID SAVANNA

The Kgalagadi Transfrontier Park is situated in the Kalahari basin, which stretches from Zimbabwe in the east to the Atlantic Ocean in the west. It is not a true desert, although in some ways it resembles one. The wider Kalahari Basin is a savanna with grassland interspersed with trees and shrubs but because of the aridity of the landscapes, it is classified as arid savanna.

Different **landscapes** or **ecozones** can be distinguished: high dunes, low dunes, plains on deep reddish sand, calcrete ridges, plains and terraces along riverbeds and grass pans on compacted whitish sand, riverbeds and pans. Elements such as soil, temperature and water have shaped the nature of the park and endemic plants and animals have developed strategies to deal with the various adversities. These adaptations are fascinating to discover.

The vegetation has adapted to life with little water and extreme temperatures, and the habitat responds according to seasons to these changes.

In years of sufficient summer rain, the grasses flourish before turning brown in the dry winter. The riverbeds are comprised of fine, alluvial clays and the perennial and tasty buffalo grass prevails. Perennial grass species such as lovegrass, gha grass and bushman grass are the most common species found on the dunes and streets. Dune reed is the dominant perennial grass on the dune crests and is essential to stabilising the dunes. The most common summer annual grass is Kalahari sour grass.

After rain, shrubs and trees flower and some bare trees sprout leaves again. Like the yellow devil's thorn, ground covers and creeping plants flourish and bloom after the first rains. Owing to the size of the reserve, rain is often localised and certain areas may receive more rain and appear greener than others.

The characteristic and most abundant trees are the prominent camelthorns (of which there are two species – the green and grey) and the shepherd's tree. Camelthorn trees are regarded as a keystone species because of their importance for the survival of many animals and other plant species. Shrubs like the three-thorns (or driedoring) and black-thorn acacias occur along the river banks and dune streets. In the south of the park, the green camelthorn is mainly confined to the ancient and dry riverbeds, but is more widespread in the wetter far north, along the dry Nossob, on the dunes and sandy plains, and into the Botswana section of the park. The grey camelthorn grows largely along the Auob River and on the dunes, while the shepherd's tree is a common sight on dune crests and slopes

The vegetation structure influences bird populations and determines the area they inhabit. The presence of trees means more tree-living birds and other animals occur in this semi-desert than in true deserts.

BIRDS OF THE KGALAGADI

Life in the Kgalagadi is complicated and birds have to deal with the scarcity of water, extreme temperatures, shortage of food and shade, and unpredictable and variable breeding conditions. Yet, birds can cover considerable distances in a short time and many species from surrounding areas take advantage of good rainfall conditions and visit until food is in short supply.

More than half of the more than 300 species recorded in the park are incidental visitors. The most recent bird census shows that **179** Kgalagadi bird species are **usually present** during both good and bad times. They are successful because they adapt to conditions, despite the semi-arid nature of the area. Some have a small distribution area, while others are abundant throughout the park. Only **86 species are truly resident** and always present. Some species are **nomads** and these birds move from place to place without regard to direction or season. Close to **30 species are annual migrants**, which means they make regular seasonal movements from their breeding areas to non-breeding areas and back again. **Vagrants** are species that do not belong in the Kgalagadi, but are **incidental visitors** when conditions are favourable. **More than 160 species are vagrants**. Most of these are waterbirds that visit the seasonal pans in the years of good rain. Others are birds that took the wrong course and one such example is the Greater Painted-Snipe.

In the past, people thought birds living in arid and semi-arid environments were pre-adapted to do so, but recent research convincingly demonstrates they have evolved physiological and behavioural traits that have allowed them to be successful in arid environments. Not all resident birds in the semi-arid Kgalagadi necessarily show spectacular or visible adaptations to this dry place since many also occur in mesic environments (moderately moist habitats). Thanks to artificial waterholes and giant trees with deep root systems in the dry riverbeds, **many mesic or near-mesic habitats occur in the Kgalagadi**. Therefore, many predators and insect feeders, which usually occur in mesic habitats do survive in the Kgalagadi.

Many of the Kgalagadi residents show behavioural adaptations and some of these behaviours are captivating to discover and observe. It is interesting to ponder the different kinds of social organisations and how they aid in the successful breeding and survival of the species, how food and feeding methods vary, how defence mechanisms play a role, and why so many migrant birds visit in summer.

Greater Painted Snipe – Incidental Visitors

Burchell's Sandgrouse

ADAPTATIONS TO THE ARID ENVIRONMENT OF THE KGALAGADI

How birds counteract heat stress (thermoregulate)

Birds that thrive in semi-arid areas can thermoregulate through certain behaviours and physiological means. Birds cannot sweat to regulate their body temperature and therefore have to apply other strategies, such as evaporative cooling, download excess body heat, reduce activity during the hottest part of the day, and minimise heat stress by flying during cooler times.

The surrounding air temperature in semi-deserts is often much higher (or much lower) than the bird's body temperature. Birds generally have a slightly higher body temperature than mammals, which allows them to forage longer before they have to retreat to shade or apply other ways of cooling down. This also ensures a steady flow of heat out of the body if the air temperature is below 40°C.

Ostriches, among others, seem to have the most remarkable ability to keep their body temperature at sub-lethal levels when the air temperature would kill most birds. Much of the success of ostriches in semi-arid and desert environments is the effectiveness of their behavioural actions in maintaining their body temperature. They apply **wing-drooping behaviour** when the air temperature becomes too high for comfort and **expose the thermal windows** that can offload excess. When the air temperature increases, they **use their wings as umbrellas** to shade their bodies and their substantial naked thighs. They orientate their long axis towards the sun, droop their wings to their sides and raise their feathers on their backs to allow the maximum airflow even in the slightest breeze to remove heat trapped over their skin surface. When temperatures drop excessively, they use **their wings as blankets** to keep warm and sit on the ground with their legs folded underneath their bodies so as not to expose their skin, and to trap warm air.

Common Ostrich Wing Drooping

Ostrich Family

Grey-backed Sparrow-lark

Cape Glossy Starling

Many diurnal (day-active) animals in the Kgalagadi seek protection from the heat by using underground burrows, where temperatures can be up to 20°C cooler than above ground, thereby selecting a cooler micro-habitat. Although birds do not usually live in burrows or underground cavities, **some species use burrows** for insulation. The Ant-eating Chat roosts in disused aardvark burrows and will retreat there if conditions becomes unbearably hot. The Spike-heeled Lark will occasionally do something similar using rodent burrows.

Some birds will **perch on a raised object** a few centimetres above the ground. Most **use shade** to offload excess heat, but others use sand to cool down because sand is a better heat conductor than air. Namaqua Doves, sandgrouse, and vultures download heat directly and quickly onto the sand by **sitting down or lying flat on a sandy surface**.

Most birds get rid of heat by **panting**, but this strategy is used sparingly because rapid breathing uses more energy. Others, such as the ostrich and sandgrouse, use **gular fluttering**. The gular area is situated at the back of the bird's mouth and is a thin-skinned chamber with a network of blood vessels. The bird pumps air in and out of the pouch by twitching the chamber's muscles while keeping its beak open. This has the same effect as panting but without the energy-intensive use of the lungs.

Huddling together is also a successful strategy for cooling down in scorching weather or retaining body heat in freezing conditions. Huddling reduces the inflow of heat into the body. This method is so effective that sandgrouse can keep their body temperature below 42°C even when the air temperature reaches 50°C.

Birds have **specialised scales** on their legs and feet, and birds with long legs often defecate on their legs to cool themselves down. This frequently occurs among storks. When it is freezing, some birds, mainly waterbirds, will conserve heat by standing on one leg or even sitting down with their beak hidden in the wing's feathers to counteract heat loss from the body.

Nests can serve as **thermal shelters**. Some of the most successful species of semi-arid places are Sociable Weavers. These birds build large,

Sociable Weaver Nest Chamber

Abdim's Stork

many-chambered nests on camelthorns. Notice that they never select the top branches of a tree to start a nest and instead choose one of the lower branches to ensure some natural shade. Amazingly, the temperature inside their nests never fluctuates more than six degrees. While temperatures outside may rise to the high 40s during the day and drop well below freezing at night, the inner nest chambers are never more than 31°C and never below 15°C. The deeper nests are the five-star units, the coolest and preferred by the veteran pairs. Sociable Weavers huddle together when it is cold and up to five can be in the same nest.

Common Ostrich

How Kgalagadi birds deal with the scarcity of water

Water is essential for all life and therefore a critical resource. Birds in the Kgalagadi overcome water scarcity in a few different ways. At least three sources are available to them: free water, which is surface water available for birds and other animals to drink; preformed water, which is water contained within the food the birds feed on; and metabolic water, which is water produced by the bird's own digestive system and other metabolic processes.

Secretarybird

Free water

Since rainwater is not readily available in the Kgalagadi, man-made **boreholes** provide life support for most animals, including birds. Owing to high water salinity at some boreholes, drinking water quality is only sometimes potable. Most seedeaters depend on drinking water daily, and they do so particularly in the mornings. Species include doves, sandgrouse, finches, sparrows and canaries. Some birds fly far distances to water, which is highly energy-consuming, but it does mean they can find untapped food sources far from water.

Small passerines with relatively poor flying power must live close to water to survive. Seedeaters such as canaries and other small birds are therefore forced to stay within six to eight kilometres of a consistent water source, thus their distribution is limited.

As seedeaters, **sandgrouse must drink regularly**. Up to 6000 sandgrouse can visit suitable waterholes in one morning, some up to 80 kilometres away. **Sandgrouse** and some **doves** visit standing water in large flocks at dawn and dusk. The former transport water soaked in their specialised belly feathers to their flightless chicks.

Grey-backed Sparrow-lark

Sandgrouse wouldn't occur in such abundance in the park were it not for the borehole water. Remarkably, these pigeon-like birds can make a round trip of up to 160 kilometres a day for a drink. Even more astonishing is that when they have chicks, the males soak their specially modified chest and belly feathers to carry water back to their young.

This water-carrying phenomenon is unique to sandgrouse. Like its other feathers, the water-carrying feathers also have barbules, but they are all spiralled and twisted when dry. When they are wet they straighten at right angles to the barbs along the flat sides of the feathers closest to the body and become a dense mat resembling velvet that acts like a sponge. Scientists estimate that in this way, each feather can hold up to 25 times its weight in water.

When a male bird enters the water it immediately fluffs and erects its breast and belly feathers, but raises its wings and tail so as not to wet them. It briefly drinks and then rocks its body back and forth or up and down in the water to wet the breast and belly feathers. Water enters by capillary action along the inside of the feathers close to the body and in this way, water is protected from spillage and wind evaporation as the bird flies back to its chicks. Some of the water will inevitably be lost, but what is left is still enough to meet the moisture needs of the chicks. Back at the nest area, the male walks to the chicks, stands erect and allows the chicks to suck and comb the feathers for water.

Preformed water in food

Preformed water includes **water absorbed from food** and encompasses birds that feed on fruits such as berries, those that feed on flesh (such as raptors), insects and other invertebrates. This is highly profitable for these species since the availability of open water does not limit their distribution.

Namaqua Sandgrouse Male Soaking its Feathers

Swallow-tailed Bee-eater

Metabolic water

Metabolic water refers to **water created inside a living organism through its metabolism**. This is water formed during the process of cellular respiration. The water produced from the metabolism of protein roughly equals the amount needed to excrete the byproduct of the metabolism of protein, which is urea in mammals. Birds excrete uric acid instead of urea and gain net water from protein metabolism. **Larks** and **some sparrows** can convert fat, carbohydrates and protein energy sources obtained from seeds into water, which is why these birds are particularly successful in arid environments.

Migratory birds must rely exclusively on metabolic water production while making non-stop flights.

Sandgrouse use body water economically by avoiding too much salt intake, and their kidneys are adapted to conserve salt and water.

The **Scaly-feathered Finch** (weaver) is the only seedeater able to survive for at least 62 days without drinking. This little bird can produce its water through specific metabolic processes and can therefore survive for a long time away from an open water source. It supplements its diet with harvester termites, which are only sometimes available.

Scaly-feathered Finch (Weaver)

Sociable Weavers Feeding

How Kgalagadi birds deal with a shortage of food

In arid environments, food supply is erratic so bird densities are low. One potential adaptation to counteract food scarcity is a reduced metabolic rate or digestion. This requires less food to fuel the bird and reduces water loss and heat production. Another adaptation is for the bird to be a food generalist, which means not being too fussy about what they eat. While insects and invertebrates may be scarce, ants and termites are always available and prolific.

Therefore, birds that eat **ants and termites** seldom have a problem finding food. Larks, Sociable Weavers and others eat both **seeds and insects**. The food provides nutrients and moisture, which make these birds ideal semi-arid dwellers.

It helps if the bird can **move around** over short and long distances (nomadism) to exploit food elsewhere when food becomes scarce. The seedeaters are generally nomadic and move about more than the predominantly insectivorous ones.

During winter, food is scarce and therefore the birds' activities (which require spending energy) are restricted to the minimum for survival. The bodies of Scaly-feathered Finches are so small that they perish quickly in extremely cold weather, but by huddling close together they conserve energy and keep each other warm. It's hard to believe that up to 12 of these tiny finches can squeeze into one of their little nests to roost. Sometimes they will even roost in an unoccupied Sociable Weaver nest, or use an old cup nest of a shrike or flycatcher and build a roof over it.

Ways in which Kgalagadi birds optimise their chances for successful breeding

Although individual species may have adaptations to reduce energy expenditure and water loss, they still have to breed. Breeding is a process that requires a lot of energy expenditure but several semi-arid adapted birds have cut corners and put almost 30 percent less energy into reproduction than birds in mesic (wetter) habitats. This can lead to a higher nestling mortality, but a higher adult survival rate offsets this. This is the case in some of the lark species.

In some species, **breeding is delayed** until after unpredictable rainfall to ensure enough food for the nestlings. This is typical of some **lark** and **weaver species**.

Cooperative breeding is often the order of the day in bird species that live in social groups, and this is a particularly successful strategy in arid areas such as the Kalahari. In this strategy, one pair of nesting birds (the alpha pair) is assisted with incubation and chick-rearing by one or several others of the same species. Food in the arid savanna is hard to find but if there are more food providers, there is a better chance for the chicks to reach adulthood.

Predation is another danger and helpers assist with territorial and nest defence. The downside of this strategy is that not all birds get to breed, but it is more critical for the species to thrive through cooperation and assistance than for the individuals to benefit.

Sociable Weavers are opportunistic breeders. Of all desert-adapted birds they have the shortest response period after the rains to start breeding. Within five days after a shower they lay eggs. When they hatch, the chicks have a significant advantage over others for food. They can rear up to four broods per season.

The individual nest chambers of Sociable Weavers are difficult to access. The tunnels leading to the breeding chambers may be up to 27 centimetres long and seven centimetres wide, while the breeding chambers are 10 to 15 centimetres in diameter. They are lined with soft materials such as feathers, fluff, wool or hair.

Cape Cobra Raiding Sociable Weavers' Nests

Sociable Weaver Nest

White-browed Sparrow-weavers live in groups of between two and 11 birds. Each group will build its nests with colonies consisting of, on average, 16 nests in a single tree. The nests are nearly always on the leeward side of a tree, between two and eight metres off the ground. Each group will have several nests; one for breeding and the others for roosting. Nests are constructed from long, dry grass stems that are bent over but not woven. It is typically wedged into the branches of a camelthorn tree.

A nest is built by breeders and helpers in about five to 30 days and maintained throughout the year. Nests consist of untidy, retort-shaped structures with two entrances, one on each side. It is used for roosting, with one bird per nest. The nest provides enough insulation for significant energy savings, paramount in an environment with extreme temperatures. Scientists reckon that the reason for the success of White-browed Sparrow-weavers to survive in unpredictable environments is also because they have adopted a **cooperative breeding strategy**. A single pair of Sparrow-weavers might struggle to find enough food for their offspring. That's probably why the birds live communally; a large group is more likely to rear young successfully. The helper birds miss out on young of their own, but the genes shared with the alpha birds' offspring will survive to the next generation.

Scaly-feathered Finches are a remarkable desert-adapted bird species. They are social birds that live in flocks of about 20 individuals, build untidy nests, and employ **cooperative breeding**. When breeding starts, the breeding pair closes one end of the nest to form a breeding chamber. The female incubates alone and the group members collaborate to feed the chicks. After fledging, the chicks will still beg and be fed by the helpers for at least a week. The breeding season generally coincides with rainfall patterns and in the Kgalagadi, it usually lasts from January to June. The breeding pair preen each other, particularly around the head, which does suggest they are monogamous (at least during the breeding season). When a new nest is built,

Double-banded Courser

Scaly-feathered Finch (Weaver)

White-browed Sparrow-weaver

White-browed Sparrow-weaver Nest

the male supplies the building material while the female constructs the nest, which she lines with soft grass heads. Incubation is short, from 10 to 12 days, and only the female performs this task but both the males and females tend to the chicks. All seedeaters have to drink regularly, but there are exceptions.

One of the best desert-adapted birds is found in the barren areas near Union's End. The beautiful **Double-banded Courser** does not need drinking water and can withstand extreme overheating. It prefers open areas and moves away from places where rain has fallen because it requires open, bare ground for good visibility. In contrast to most other birds, it breeds throughout the year, irrespective of conditions, laying a single egg up to four times a year on exposed ground and in the full sun. Ground temperatures in the Kalahari can rise to 70°C, much higher than the air temperature a metre or so above the ground. The male and female take turns to prevent the egg from being cooked by the sun during incubation. How they regulate the incubating temperature to stay constant is genuinely remarkable. When the ambient temperature is below 30°C, they incubate it; if the ambient temperature is higher they shade it. If the temperature exceeds 36°C, they incubate it to withdraw heat. Each parent has a turn in the sun to shade or incubate the egg, while the other one cools off or rests in the shade of a tree, where it loses excess heat before returning to the egg after an hour.

Juvenile Lanner Falcon

KGALAGADI BIRD SPECIES

RAPTORS OR CARNIVOROUS BIRDS

All raptors or birds of prey are meat eaters or carnivores. They are primarily large to giant in size, but a few are small to medium. All have substantial, sharply hooked bills and relatively large eyes that are often red, yellow or orange. Their feet are strong with stout, sharply curved claws enabling them to grasp live prey. Their wings are well developed, primarily broad and long for soaring; others are short for manoeuvrability; and others are pointed for speed. Raptors catch their prey actively, but are opportunists that scavenge on carrion when the opportunity arises. Owls are also raptors because they are carnivorous, have hooked beaks, strong feet, sharp talons and keen eyesight. However, owls (Strigidae and Tytonidae) are not closely related to the other families of raptors, which are the Sagittariidae, Accipitridae and Falconidae. The Kgalagadi Transfrontier Park has a surprising number and density of raptor species, even more so than other reserves with a far favourable climate and better plant cover where you would expect to encounter plenty. This higher density results from the enormous surface area covered by the park. The surrounding region is sparsely populated by humans, resulting in a lower impact on raptor numbers. The large rodent population in the park also contributes to the excellent raptor population.

Hunting Pale-chanting Goshawk

Pigmy Falcon Pair

Enrico Liebenberg

DIURNAL TERRESTRIAL RAPTORS OR BIRDS OF PREY

ONE OF ITS KIND

Family: Sagittariidae

Number of species: 1

Sagittariidae is a family of raptors with only one living species. It is diurnal and hunts on the ground. Secretarybirds are unusual birds of prey and quite unlike any other raptor in the world as they have an eagle-like bill and long legs with shortish feet, but no talons.

Although secretarybirds are found over an extensive range, the results of localised surveys suggest the total population is experiencing a rapid decline, probably because of habitat degradation.

SECRETARYBIRD ★

Sekretarisvoël

Sagittarius serpentarius

Although secretarybirds are widespread, they are uncommon and a sighting is special. They seldom fly but soar like vultures on broad wings to great heights once in the air. They usually hunt in pairs. Look out for them in open areas, particularly in the drainage line of the Auob riverbed near Auchterlonie. There they stride slowly across the veld with their long crests waving in the breeze as they search for prey on the ground.

They catch smaller prey items with their bills, but larger prey is subdued by stamping on it with their feet, wings held open. Prey consists of insects, amphibians, reptiles, rodents, hares, young birds and eggs. They have a hard knob of skin on the underside of each foot that they use to deliver a powerful and accurate blow to stun their prey. When killing a snake, they stamp on it until it is completely lifeless. They swallow their prey whole.

Secretarybirds cannot perch; rather they nest and roost on trees. They build their nests on top of thorn trees that have a flattish crown. Courtship flights are performed on the wing. Breeding can take place at any time of year but tends to be late in the dry season.

DIURNAL AERIAL RAPTORS OR BIRDS OF PREY

ACCIPITERS

Family: Accipitridae

Number of species: 19

The Accipitridae are the bigger flesh-eating birds and include the scavenging vultures. The eagles are the butchers of the bird world, in that they use their talons to catch and kill their prey. All have firmly hooked bills and powerful feet with sharp talons typical of all raptors, but the size, appearance and behaviour varies among the different species. In this way, each species fills a particular niche and thus minimises competition. Vultures are essential as they serve as avian undertakers and rarely kill their prey.

WHITE-BACKED VULTURE ★

Witrugaasvoël

Gyps africanus

These vultures are aggressive birds that arrive in large numbers at carcasses and feed mainly on the softer parts of large mammals and any other carrion, bone splinters and tender parts. Look out for nests in the Auob riverbed in the region of Dalkeith, the 13th and 14th boreholes.

THE VULTURES

Vultures are large, carrion-feeding birds with strong, curved bills. Most of them have bare necks and heads. When the air has heated sufficiently in the morning to cause thermals, they take to the wing to look for carcasses over a vast area. The first one to notice potential food will fly down and the others will follow it in a spiralling flight. Vultures often bathe and sun themselves at a waterhole at midday and sometimes in significant numbers. They also like to dust-bathe.

Although the large White-backed Vulture is common in the Kgalagadi Transfrontier Park, it is threatened with extinction elsewhere. This is because of habitat loss and scarcity; poisoning for the 'muti' (informal medicine) trade also contributes to its decline.

Their colour varies from a uniform dark-brown to off-white, while the eyes are dark-brown. It is a species that breeds and roosts in tall trees. The nest is a stick platform usually on top of the crown of a big camelthorn tree. Eggs are laid from April to July and hatch in 56 to 58 days and remain dependent on the parents for four to five months.

LAPPET-FACED VULTURE ★

Swartaasvoël

Torgos tracheliotos

Expect to see this aggressive latecomer at a carcass where it scares off other smaller vultures by its sheer size. It is often seen close to water, where it drinks and suns itself with its wings outstretched.

The giant Lappet-faced Vulture is a widespread but threatened species. The desert conditions of the Kgalagadi create an ideal habitat for these scavengers that prefer large areas of open land with minimal grass cover.

This vulture is easily recognised by its heavy, reddish-to-pink naked head and wrinkled, loose folded skin on the sides of its neck. Adults have a brown-and-white-streaked chest and baggy white leggings while immatures are all brown.

In flight, the broad and long wings, white leggings and small white lines at the front of the wings are diagnostic.

With its massive bill it can rip open a carcass and feed on tougher body parts such as the skin, ligament and bone. It finds carcasses by watching other birds and therefore much time is spent gliding and soaring. Despite being mainly a scavenger, it does kill prey such as hares and feed on emerging winged termites.

WHITE-HEADED VULTURE

Witkopaasvoël

Trigonoceps occipitalis

Large. Uncommon. Distribution limited to the far north. Resembles the Lappet-faced Vulture.

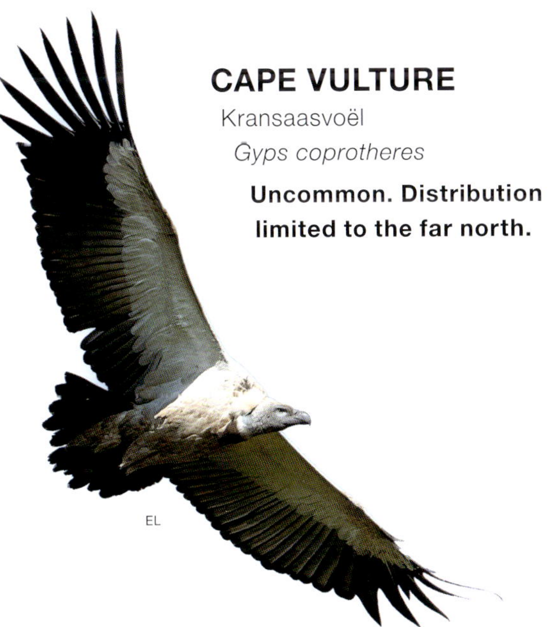

EL

CAPE VULTURE

Kransaasvoël

Gyps coprotheres

Uncommon. Distribution limited to the far north.

EAGLES

Assertive and aggressive hunters, these medium- to giant raptors (also called true eagles) all have fully feathered legs. Some are resident but others are migratory. The most sought-after eagles for birders visiting the Kgalagadi include the Martial and Tawny Eagles.

MARTIAL EAGLE ★

Breëkoparend

Polemaetus bellicosus

Martial Eagles are widespread but not numerous and can be seen anywhere in the Kgalagadi. They usually hunt from great heights while soaring but also hunt from perches. Look for a nesting site on the crown of a tall camelthorn with a Sociable Weaver nest about 6.5 kilometres from the confluence on the southern banks of the Nossob River. The nest is a large stick bowl high up in trees and tends to be used for consecutive years.

Martial Eagles are the largest of the African eagles. They are heavily persecuted outside conservation areas so the park is a stronghold for this magnificent eagle. Like other avian predatory birds high up in the food chain, Martial Eagles have a long life expectancy and a slow reproduction rate.

Recognise this eagle by looking for the dark-brown head, upperpart and breast; white underparts with dark-brown spots; legs with white-feathered leggings. The juvenile's overall appearance is pale, with grey above and pure white breast and unmarked leggings.

They are rapacious and versatile hunters that mostly hunt from great heights while soaring and spotting potential prey up to six kilometres away. With strong bodies and exceptionally powerful claws, Martial Eagles take big prey, which includes includes mammals such as smaller antelope, hares, ground squirrels, African wild cats, mongooses and larger birds, even ones as massive as the Kori Bustard.

They nest in winter and rear only one chick at a time. The offspring remains dependent for a very long while.

TAWNY EAGLE ★

Roofarend

Aquila rapax

The most frequently seen true eagles in the Kgalagadi are the Tawny Eagles. These eagles are typical savanna raptors that generally occur in pairs occupying a permanent territory. Tawny Eagles are monogamous, pair for life and breed once a year.

These eagles have a shaggy appearance, rounded heads and fully feathered legs. Their plumage can vary from streaked dark-brown to pale buff (blond), but all have some tawny (rufous brown) colour.

Tawny Eagles tend to perch or fly in open arid savanna landscapes. As opportunistic and rapacious hunters, they take a variety of prey, ranging from medium-sized mammals, reptiles and birds (sometimes taken in flight) to insects. They are also scavengers and usually the first to arrive at a carcass. They are known to pirate other birds and obtain a fair percentage of their prey in this way. They even steal prey items from the talons or bills of flying Bateleurs and snatch fledgelings from nests. They often join Lanner Falcons in trees at waterholes, waiting for birds to come to drink.

BOOTED EAGLE

Dwergarend

Hieraaetus pennatus

Smallish; unobtrusive; seen alone or in a pair. Non-breeding migrant from Europe; far northeast of the park and Botswana.

EL

Enrico Liebenberg

BATELEUR ★

Berghaan

Terathopius ecaudatus

Look for Bateleurs soaring high in the sky, gently rocking from side to side. You may also find them at any of the various waterholes. They arrive late in the morning and spend a long time sunbathing with their wings open and the body curved forward or quenching their thirst.

Juvenile

The Bateleur is an atypical snake eagle that can easily be mistaken for one of the true eagles. Unlike true eagles, it has unfeathered lower legs, feeds on various small animals and is often the first to discover carrion. Adult birds are beautiful with their black, white, grey and chestnut feathers, and red faces, legs and feet with short toes. The immature birds are brown and easily confused with the Brown Snake Eagle as they both have bare legs, a large, rounded head, grey beak and cere.

The Bateleur is a remarkable raptor and one of the most magnificent fliers in the African sky. Well known for its interesting flying technique, it can soar with scarcely a wingbeat over long distances, reportedly up to 300 kilometres in a day, looking for food. Its name is derived from the French word for a tightrope walker because of its characteristic flight action of gently rocking from side to side.

These birds are endangered outside conservation areas, but fortunately they are pretty common in the Kgalagadi. Every pair has its own specific territory. They build their relatively small platform of stick nests high up in trees and lay only one egg at a time. The egg takes 55 days to hatch – the most extended incubation period of any African eagle. Juvenile birds are dull brown and take up to eight years to mature.

On sunny days, Bateleurs start soaring from about nine o'clock in the morning. On rainy and overcast days they do not fly as they rely on thermals and on such days they perch high up in trees. Although Bateleurs are primarily scavengers they do hunt birds, small mammals, reptiles and even the eggs of ground-nesting birds.

Bateleurs drink regularly but also visit waterholes for other purposes. They arrive late in the morning and can spend a long time sunbathing with their wings open and the body curved forward. They may lie flat on their tummies, allowing ants to crawl over their feathers. When they eventually get up, they shake their feathers, startling the ants, which then secrete formic acid, which is said to protect them against parasites.

SNAKE EAGLES

Snake eagles are medium- to large-sized raptors, but differ from other species because of their large, rounded heads, long, unfeathered but heavily scaled legs and short toes. They have conspicuous large yellow eyes, are specialist snake killers, and prey almost entirely on these reptiles. The Black-chested and Brown Snake Eagle are two species found in the Kgalagadi Transfrontier Park.

BLACK-CHESTED SNAKE EAGLE ★

Swartborsslangarend

Circaetus pectoralis

Black-chested Snake Eagles are common in the park and can be seen resting on exposed perches or flying very high in the sky. They prefer to hunt while soaring. Watch out for their small nests that tower above in trees.

Black-chested Snake Eagles are the most common of the two species. They are good-looking raptors with their head and breast dark, while the unspotted underparts are white. It is easy to identify them when they perch or fly.

They prefer to hunt while soaring and drop down on their prey like a parachute and grab it behind the head, crushing it with their short, powerful feet. They also hover and hunt from a perch. Snakes are often half ingested, with the tails protruding from their bills. When feeding their young, big snakes are carried in the eagle's talons. The chicks pull out half-ingested snakes and swallow them whole.

BROWN SNAKE EAGLE ★

Bruinslangarend

Circaetus cinereus

The Brown Snake Eagle is larger than the Black-chested Snake Eagle and occurs throughout the park. It is less numerous than the black-chested one. It frequently hunts from a perch, killing and swallowing prey on the ground. More significant prey species, such as the Cape cobra may take some effort to subdue. It sometimes uses Sociable Weavers' nests as perches or to roost.

With its overall dark-brown plumage, the Brown Snake Eagle can easily be confused with various large brown eagles or the juvenile Black-chested Snake Eagle. Look at their eyes and legs. The eyes are large, round and intensely yellow. The lower legs are grey-white and not feathered but scaled.

KITES

Kites are small to medium raptors with long wings and are all magnificent flyers. However, their behaviour and hunting strategies vary from species to species.

BLACK-WINGED KITE ★

Blouvalk

Elanus caeruleus

The Kgalagadi habitat, with its open spaces and wealth of rodents, is ideally suited for these handsome raptors, and they are a pretty common sighting. Hunting birds perch conspicuously on branches along most of the roads. When excited, they wag their tails up and down and at dusk they often hover with their wings held high above their back.

Black-winged Kites can be identified by their grey backs, white bellies and black patches on the shoulders and the adults have red eyes. They are highly prey-specific, with rodents at the top of the list, but they also take shrews, birds, reptiles and insects. Although they hunt singly, non-breeding birds roost communally at night, sometimes in big groups. In the mornings, each individual flies out to its specific hunting area for the day. They breed throughout the year depending on climatic conditions. It is interesting to note that the male is responsible for feeding the nestlings.

YELLOW-BILLED KITE

Geelbekwou

Milvus aegyptius

Look for Yellow-billed Kites in summer after good rains when they arrive in vast numbers to utilise the temporary abundance of insects, especially termite alates. They perch high up in trees, scanning the surroundings for possible prey or pursuing prey in flight. Juveniles may be mistaken for Black Kites because of their dark bills. Huge flocks sometimes gather at waterholes to drink or just relax.

The dark-brown body, forked tail, yellow bill and legs are identifying features of Yellow-billed Kites. They are migratory birds from further north in Africa that arrive in South Africa during early spring, where they start breeding soon after arrival. They are gregarious when not breeding but form pairs during nesting. These excellent flyers are incredibly nimble in flight, sweeping down to pick up prey or catch prey in flight. It is interesting to note that flying insects are caught with their talons. As opportunists, they feed on a variety of animal matter and even rob other raptors of prey and may steal food from a picnic table.

BLACK KITE

Swartwou

Milvus migrans

Uncommon; closely related to Yellow-billed Kites and look similar; intra-African migrants; do not breed here; huge flocks follow insect (termite) outbreaks in summer.

BUZZARDS

Buzzards are medium to large robust raptors with broad wings. Some species could be confused with brown eagles but they all have bare lower legs. They can soar well but generally hunt from a perch.

COMMON (STEPPE) BUZZARD ★

Bruinjakkalsvoël

Buteo buteo

These raptors are common in the Kgalagadi during wet summer months. They favour exposed perches but also hunt soaring. They can easily be confused with Brown Snake Eagles or juvenile Black-chested Snake Eagles, but their legs are shorter with unfeathered lower parts, and the eyes are smaller and darker.

Common Buzzards are Palearctic non-breeding migrants from the far northern parts of Eurasia. It is one of southern Africa's most common medium-sized summer-visiting raptors. They take smaller prey than similar eagles. Insects make up a significant part of their diet; however, they do also catch small birds, mammals and reptiles. Their back is almost uniformly brown but the underpart's plumage is highly variable, from dark, chocolate-brown to pale with various markings.

JACKAL BUZZARD

Rooiborsjakkalsvoël

Buteo rufofuscus

Although the Jackal Buzzard is a common resident in the park, it is not seen as often as many other raptors.

SPARROWHAWKS AND GOSHAWKS

Sparrowhawks and goshawks belong to the genus Accipiter, the largest genus of diurnal birds of prey. They all have short, rounded wings, long tails, long legs, and thin, long toes with sharp claws. These characteristics make the smaller sparrowhawks and goshawks ideal for pursuing birds in areas with trees. The medium-sized goshawks are birds of prey in open savanna and have a more cosmopolitan diet. The little sparrowhawk is an occasional vagrant but hunts largely from a perch.

Melanistic Morph

GABAR GOSHAWK ★

Witkruissperwer

Micronisus gabar

Look out for this widespread raptor in areas with trees. It usually occurs in pairs but is difficult to spot as it prefers dense tree canopies for perching. Occasionally it may sit in the open. Gabar Goshawks spend time at the water, sometimes standing for long periods in pools.

Juvenile

The grey breast distinguishes the Gabar Goshawks from other similar-looking raptors with barred undersides. Juveniles have dark-brown upperparts with a chest streaked with brown and a white belly with fine brown bars. About 15 percent of Gabar Goshawks are melanistic and are black with white barring on the wings and tail.

Gabar Goshawks are bold hunters catching prey from a perch or in flight, often larger than themselves and they are robbers of other birds' nests. They also take small mammals, reptiles and insects.

Juvenile

PALE CHANTING GOSHAWK ★

Bleeksingvalk

Melierax canorus

The Pale Chanting Goshawk is one of the icons of the Kalahari. It occurs along almost all roads in the park and is easy to recognise with its long orange-red legs, cere and bill and pale grey plumage with fine barring on its belly, flanks and undertail.

The Pale Chanting Goshawk often soars, perches or even walks on the ground. Sometimes it spends time at water. Immature birds take a long time to mature and look completely different with their brown backs and streakily striped undersides, but they also have pale yellow eyes and pale orange ceres, legs and feet.

If you see a Pale Chanting Goshawk on the ground, stop and observe. They are opportunistic and may stay near a foraging honey badger to snatch up rodents disturbed by the digging badger. Its varied diet includes snakes and other reptiles, mammals and insects. Its hunting strategies may seem ungainly but it is a successful hunter. Its melodious piping call is typical of the Kgalagadi.

SHIKRA

Gebande Sperwer

Accipiter badius

The small Shikra is uncommon and usually perches conspicuously, is very vocal and hunts from a perch. It is a resident and a nomad.

The Shikra is a small goshawk recognised by the blueish-grey upperparts and white underparts finely barred with reddish-brown up to the throat. The cream undertail has four black bars. The eyes are red, the bill-sheath is orange-yellow and the bill is black. The juveniles are brown above and white below, mottled and barred with reddish-brown. The Shikra feeds on lizards and small animals.

AFRICAN HARRIER-HAWK

Kaalwangvalk

Polyboroides typus

The African Harrier-Hawk is a medium-sized greyish raptor with a long but small angular head. It is often seen along the 13th and 14th borehole loops along the upper Auob riverbed, clumsily clambering and foraging about on cliffs and in trees.

The bare yellow face sometimes flushes red when excited. It has long, slender yellow legs, a white-banded black tail and an underwing pattern. In flight, these birds have broad wings, which is characteristic of the species. The immature is blotchy brown with yellow-green facial skin and barred flight feathers. An unusual trait of this species is its flexible legs, which appear double-jointed and enable it to reach into otherwise inaccessible holes and cracks for prey.

Their ability to climb using their wings and feet and long, flexible legs enable these birds to raid the nests of cavity-nesters such as barbets, Palm Swifts and Wood-hoopoes for fledgelings and robbing weaver nests. They are also known to feed on frogs, insects and reptiles.

HARRIER-HAWKS

There are only two closely related species called harrier-hawks, one in Africa and the other in Madagascar. Harrier-hawks are raptors but are best placed in their own grouping. Some birders group them with goshawks and sparrowhawks, while others see them as closer related to the harriers.

FALCONS AND KESTRELS – DIURNAL AND AERIAL

Family: Falconidae

Number of species: 5

Falcons and kestrels are medium- to small-sized birds with long, pointed wings and tails. Their toes are long and sharp and they have strong claws. They hunt by stooping or hovering. Their strongly hooked bill is notched or toothed behind the tip.

FALCONS

Falcons are the speedsters of the bird world and rely on that speed to catch their main prey, which is birds.

LANNER FALCON ★

Edelvalk

Falco biarmicus

Lanner Falcons are common in the Kgalagadi. Look for them at waterholes where flocks of birds are drinking with camelthorn trees growing close by. They usually perch unobtrusively high in the canopy of a tree and surprise the birds drinking at the waterhole. Dalkeith and 14th borehole loops in the Auob, Cubitje Quap, Marie se Gat and Polentswa waterholes are some of the most productive for watching Lanner Falcons.

Juvenile

The adult's rufous crown, grey upperparts and pinkish-buff underparts are diagnostic. Look for the black line below the eyes, the yellow eye ring, and the yellow cere and legs. The juvenile also has a rufous crown but is paler and brown above and heavily streaked with brown buff breasts.

Lanner Falcons are the largest falcons in the area.

They have a stocky build, are extremely powerful and are excellent flyers. They spread their tails in flight and often hunt in pairs. They usually perch close to the water in high trees where birds come to drink, patiently waiting until big flocks arrive before they strike. Flying termites are snatched and eaten in flight but they take other insects on the ground. They also pirate prey from other raptors and raid bird nests.

RED-NECKED FALCON

Rooinekvalk

Falco chicquera

Look for the Red-necked Falcons in the tree-lined Nossob and Auob rivers. They seldom perch in the open and seldom seen. They sometimes spend some time on the ground near a waterhole. However, they are also uncommon residents.

Red-necked Falcons are beautiful raptors of southern Africa's arid, western savanna regions. This slender, small raptor's rich chestnut crown and nape are diagnostic. The back is blue-grey and the lower underside is white with distinctive black bars. As a fast flyer this bird-catcher chases its prey at high speed, often for hundreds of metres.

Juvenile

PYGMY FALCON ★

Dwergvalk

Polihierax semitorquatus

The Pygmy Falcon's range coincides with that of the Sociable Weaver as it uses the nest chambers of these birds to roost and breed. Look for these iconic birds near the enormous nests of Sociable Weavers. Nest chambers occupied by Pygmy Falcons are recognisable by a white coating of droppings at the entrance.

Not many parks in southern Africa are home to the largest raptor, the Martial Eagle, and the smallest, the Pygmy Falcon. Both are regular sightings in the Kgalagadi. The minute Pygmy Falcon resembles a Fiscal or Lesser Grey Shrike, but can be distinguished by its hooked bill and pinkish-orange legs. It is grey above and white below, but the female has a chestnut back and is bigger than the male. It hunts from a perch and catches its prey on the ground.

Enrico Liebenberg

A common question is whether these raptors will take some of their hosts' nestlings and they do, but only on rare occasions. Their main prey consists of insects and small reptiles and, less often, rodents and birds.

KESTRELS

Kestrels belong to the same family as the falcons but differ in a few respects. Kestrels make less use of speed to catch prey and hunt from perches or by hovering.

ROCK KESTREL

Kransvalk

Falco rupicolus

Look out for these raptors perching on exposed perches or hovering. They can be spotted next to the road, either on a perch or on the ground. They feed on small mammals, reptiles, insects and small birds.

Rock Kestrels are small raptors with rufous, spotted bodies and grey heads. They are widespread and prefer open areas close to rocky outcrops. They occur solitary or in pairs and are not gregarious like other kestrels. They fly with rapid wingbeats and hover frequently, especially when the wind blows. They drop down to their prey by parachuting in stages or may catch small birds in flight by fast stooping. They also hunt from a perch.

Enrico Liebenberg

GREATER KESTREL ★

Grootrooivalk

Falco rupicoloides

This clumsy-looking raptor is a regular sight along all the parks' roads, even the dune roads, where it sits on suitable perches for long periods. They catch prey on the ground and small birds in flight.

The heavily streaked, brown Greater Kestrel is a common resident of arid regions such as the Kalahari. Younger birds have dark-brown eyes but mature birds have noticeable ivory-white irises. Its diet consists mainly arthropods, although it also catches small mammals, reptiles and birds. It usually hunts from a perch, such as dry branches and even low objects such as termite mounds or rocks. Sometimes it also hovers.

NOCTURNAL RAPTORS – OWLS AND OWLETS

Two owl families can be distinguished. The Barn Owl belongs to one family and the rest are typical owls. Owls have particular adaptations to hunt at night: they all have superb night vision; their hearing is highly acute (some species can catch prey relying on their hearing alone) and their flight is silent so potential prey does not hear them approaching. All owls have binocular vision. The eyes are virtually immobile and to compensate, the neck is remarkably flexible – it can turn more than 180 degrees in either direction, allowing it to look backwards. Prey is caught with their sharp talons and swallowed whole. The undigested remains such as bones and hair or feathers are regurgitated as pellets. In Nossob Rest Camp, five different species can occasionally be seen or heard.

BARN OWLS

Family: Tytonidae
Number of species: 1

These medium- to large-sized owls have elongated, heart-shaped faces. Their bills are long and slender and their eyes are relatively small and always dark in colour.

WESTERN BARN OWL ★

Nonnetjie-uil

Tyto alba

The widespread Western Barn Owl is a resident species in the park. It is strictly nocturnal and hunts from a perch or by flying slowly over suitable hunting grounds to locate prey. It is a specialist rodent killer but other smaller vertebrates and insects are also taken. It breeds in cavities in cliffs and trees and Sociable Weavers' nests. It has adapted well to built-up areas and one can expect to hear its screeching call at night in the Nossob Camp.

Enrico Liebenberg

TYPICAL OWLS

Family: Strigidae

Number of species: 5

Five species of typical owls, ranging from small to large, occur in the Kgalagadi. Their bills are short and strong and their eyes are huge and often yellow or orange. Their ear openings are asymmetrical. Although well represented, owls are not easy to see because of their camouflage and daytime immobility. As owls are mainly arboreal, look carefully in or under large trees next to the road and in the camps.

VERREAUX'S EAGLE-OWL ★

Reuse-ooruil

Bubo lacteus

The magnificent Verreaux's Eagle-Owl is the nocturnal equivalent of the diurnal Martial Eagle. They often nest on top of the enormous Sociable Weavers' nest or roost in their favourite sleeping tree. Scan the large camelthorn trees beside the road, especially near Twee Rivieren.

The Verreaux's Eagle-Owl preys on various larger creatures such as springhares, hares, rodents, small carnivores and birds such as korhaans, raptors, nestlings of raptors and even small birds. Their call is a deep and booming 'hru hru, hru-hru-hru'.

Juvenile

SOUTHERN WHITE-FACED SCOPS OWL ★

Witwanguil

Ptilopsis granti

▾ The Southern White-faced Scops Owl prefers dry regions and is the most common and widespread owl in the park. They often roost in pairs and may use the same perch day after day. They are generally found roosting in Nossob camp.

The White-faced Scops Owl feeds mainly on rodents but also catches arthropods and birds. Look for them perching in trees and in the rest camps. Characteristic features are a white face with a black border and orange eyes. When disturbed, it elongates its body, raises its ear tufts and closes its eyes to slits.

SPOTTED EAGLE-OWL ★

Gevlekte Ooruil

Bubo africanus

▴ Sightings of Spotted Eagle-Owls during the day are unpredictable as they do not always roost in trees by day and are known to roost on the ground, often next to a tree stem, and on rocks and ledges. It is territorial and one can expect to see it several times on the same perch or in the same vicinity. They tend to shelter in the caves of the calcareous outcrops next to the dry riverbeds. If you see one during the day, you will notice the eyes are half closed and the ear tufts are erect, which is a form of camouflage.

The second largest owl in the Kalahari is the Spotted Eagle-Owl, an opportunistic bird of prey with a cosmopolitan diet consisting of rodents, beetles, scorpions, birds and even bats. With its enormous rodent population in the park, mice make up a high percentage of their diet.

AFRICAN SCOPS OWL ★

Skopsuil

Otus senegalensis

▾ The African Skops Owl is often seen in rest camps and tends to roost at the same place day after day. During sunlight hours, it perches against a stem or branch with the body elongated, ear tufts raised and eyes closed to narrow slits. In this posture it resembles a dead branch and is particularly difficult to spot.

The African Scops Owl is the smallest of the Kalahari owls. It is a master of camouflage and preys primarily on insects and scorpions, but it does also catch small vertebrates. Its call is a continuous ventriloquial 'prrrup prrrup prrrup'.

PEARL-SPOTTED OWLET ★

Witkoluil

Glaucidium perlatum

▴ Pearl-spotted Owlets are partly diurnal and do not conceal themselves like other owls do. Their loud, penetrating whistling calls can be heard during the day and night. Unlike most other owls, these beauties will stare at you with wide, open eyes. They are usually seen in the Mata Mata camp.

Although they are the smallest of all owls, they are aggressive and bold hunters of birds, rodents and insects. Their strong feet enable them to catch prey larger than themselves.

TERRESTRIAL BIRDS WITH LONG LEGS

Terrestrial birds stay primarily on the ground foraging and generally nesting and roosting on the ground or low in shrubbery. When threatened, these birds will freeze, walk or run instead of taking flight. While ostriches are naturally flightless, others are reluctant flyers that may need help to fly long distances efficiently. Most terrestrial birds that do fly stay low above the ground or close to cover when flying and typically fly only in short, frantic bursts rather than long distances. Terrestrial birds are also known as land birds or ground birds. Terrestrial birds included in this group include ostriches, storks, bustards, korhaans, thick-knees, coursers, lapwings, plovers and guineafowls. This is an arbitrary grouping and the birds are not necessarily related.

COMMON OSTRICH

Family: Struthionidae

Number of species: 1

There is only one representative for this family. It is flightless with soft drooping feathers.

COMMON OSTRICH ★

Volstruis

Struthio camelus

Ostriches are a regular sighting, both in the riverbeds and on the dunes.

The unique Common Ostrich is the largest and heaviest living bird in the world. It cannot fly even though it has a wingspan of up to two metres. It has the largest eyes of any land animal (measuring 5 cm across) and can see objects as far as 3.5 kilometres away but its brain is as small as a walnut. All in all, it is exceptionally well adapted to the severe conditions of the arid savanna of the Kgalagadi.

The male has black plumage with white wings and tail and the female is a dull brownish-grey. The barbules of the feathers are not interlocking

and are therefore useless for flying purposes as there are no tiny barbs to form an air-resistant unit as needed by flying birds. The feathers are, however, used for communication and to regulate temperature. Adults perform elaborate wing displays as a distraction when breeding or during courtship. When running, they use their wings as rudders for stability and manoeuvrability.

The excessively long neck helps ostriches to spot predators from afar. Despite their colossal size, adults can run incredibly fast and only speedsters like cheetahs can catch them. The scaly pre-historic feet have only two toes instead of four, like other birds, and these assist in their fast running.

Ostriches are almost entirely vegetarian and graze with heads held low. They have three stomachs and will swallow pebbles to help with digestion. Another unique attribute is that they are the only birds that pass urine separately from solid waste.

Ostrich eggs are the largest eggs on the planet. They nest on the ground and incubate some 20 eggs. Males and females take turns incubating the eggs while perfectly blending into the background. The male takes the night shift and the female incubates during the day. Juveniles, their bodies covered with black-and-white bristles overlying buff down, often accompany pairs. The chicks are incredibly vulnerable and fall prey to mammal predators and big raptors.

Ostriches love to dust-bathe, which involves getting dust between their feathers to help absorb excess oils. It is an essential part of bird grooming.

STORKS

Family: Ciconiidae

Number of species: 3

Storks are a group of big birds with long necks, long legs and long, straight and pointed bills. Unlike herons, they fly with their necks outstretched. Most species are mainly aquatic and absent or uncommon in arid regions. Good rains in the Kgalagadi may trigger an influx of a few stork species favouring grassland and swamped grassland.

ABDIM'S STORK

Kleinswartooievaar

Ciconia abdimii

Abdim's Storks visit the Kgalagadi only in midsummer after good rains, when they arrive in enormous flocks. They are highly nomadic seasonal infra-African non-breeding migrants from the northern regions of Africa.

These small storks, with their purplish gloss black backs and white rump and lower back, can be seen foraging in flocks in grassland. They feed mainly on larger insects but also smaller vertebrates. Huge flocks often spend some leisure time at waterholes and they roost in trees.

WHITE STORK

Witooievaar

Ciconia Ciconia

Look out for White Storks along the river valleys in high summer after good rains.

In the Kgalagadi, these large black and white birds with red legs and bills can be seen foraging among flocks of Abdim's Storks. The migratory White Storks frequently mix with other visiting storks to share any temporary abundance of prey during prolific wet periods. White Storks migrate from Eurasia to areas where good rain has fallen.

MARABOU STORK

Maraboe

Leptoptilus crumenifer

Marabou Storks are uncommon residents and are only occasionally seen north of Polentswa.

The Marabou Stork is an adaptable feeder that also scavenges. It is the largest of all the storks.

BUSTARDS AND KORHAANS

Family: Otididae

Number of species: 5

In the Kgalagadi, this family is represented by three prominent species: the Kori Bustard, the Northern Black Korhaan and the Red-crested Korhaan. The Karoo Korhaan and Ludwig's Bustard are uncommon and seldom seen. Being terrestrial (the name bustard means birds that walk), all three species are cryptically coloured to blend in with their environment, have longish legs with three short, forward-pointing toes and are reluctant to fly. Their main attraction is their impressive and spectacular displays during the breeding season. The Northern Black Korhaan is common but the Kori Bustard is the star species.

KORI BUSTARD ★

Gompou

Ardeotis kori

They prefer vast open grassland and often walk in dry riverbeds. You will also find them in lightly wooded areas where they can be seen walking sedately and slowly, looking for food. They are sensitive to vehicles and usually move away when a car is too close for comfort.

The Kori Bustard is the heaviest bird in southern Africa capable of flying. This impressive bird is frequently mistaken for a small antelope from a distance and when walking in tall grass owing to its size and colouring. It flies reluctantly because of its body mass (up to 19 kg), but it is all power and grace once in flight. Kori bustards are one of the few birds that sit on their knees while drinking and they use a sucking motion rather than scooping the water up, as most birds do.

Like the other family members, the males display spectacular displays during the breeding period. Males fluff out their neck and head feathers and inflate the necks while the tails are raised over the back. Kori Bustards do not form permanent pair bonds. Males display at a site known as a 'lek' and females are attracted to his 'lek' by his impressive display. Sometimes females may exhibit this posture when there are chicks to distract the attention of potential enemies.

These birds forage for insects, smaller vertebrates, seeds and other plant material but also eat acacia gum, hence the Afrikaans name gompou (which translates as tree gum bustard). They tend to forage alone or in pairs, but can gather in greater numbers at a good food source. Although they are not regular nomads, they will move away when food gets scarce.

NORTHERN BLACK KORHAAN ★

Witvlerkkorhaan

Afrotis afraoides

The Black Korhaan is a Kalahari icon that is regularly seen in the dunes along the dune roads. They sometimes venture onto the dry riverbeds where they can be best observed.

The Northern Black Korhaan is endemic to southern Africa and the male is the most conspicuous bird in the Kgalagadi dunes, both in appearance and behaviour. It has striking black-and-white markings, yellow legs, an orange bill and a finely barred back. A raucous cackle always accompanies the spectacle of the male. It displays from a termite mound or rock or while cruising around in flight before descending slowly with rapidly flapping wings and dangling yellow legs, with the tempo of the calls increasing before landing. One can hear its call day and night. The female is inconspicuous and secretive. They feed mainly on insects such as termites, grasshoppers, beetles and plant products such as seeds.

♂

♀

RED-CRESTED KORHAAN

Boskorhaan

Lophotis ruficrista

▸ The Red-crested Korhaan draws attention by its clicking and piping calls. If you find a calling male, treat yourself and stay to watch as a spectacular flight often follows the call. The displaying male exposes its red crest, flies straight into the air and then tumbles down as if it has been shot but opens its wings just before it hits the ground. The male displays to multiple females that incubate the one to two eggs and raise the chicks.

These birds are omnivorous, feeding on invertebrates, especially termites, beetles, grasshoppers and plant matter, particularly seeds and fruit. It forages on the ground and picks up food items with its bill.

Red-crested Korhaans are endemic to southern Africa and prefer savanna-like areas. Despite being residents, they are uncommon in the Kgalagadi.

Jaco Powell

LUDWIG'S BUSTARD

Ludwigpou

Neotis ludwigii

◂ Uncommon; nomadic; nomadic resident seldom seen.

KAROO KORHAAN

Vaalkorhaan

Eupodotis vigorsii

▾ Uncommon; seldom seen; found in extreme south in stony and sparsely vegetated areas near Twee Rivieren.

THICK-KNEES

Family: Burhinidae

Number of species: 1

Thick-knees are terrestrial birds that forage at night. They have cryptic brown plumage, long yellow legs and big yellow eyes. Only one species, the Spotted Thick-Knee, occurs in the Kgalagadi.

SPOTTED THICK-KNEE ★

Gewone Dikkop

Burhinus capensis

The Spotted Thick-Knee is a resident of the Kgalagadi but is not often seen. During the day, it crouches or stands inconspicuously in the shade of a tree or shrub. Shady camel-thorns along the Auob are an excellent place to look for them. They are sedentary and seen in pairs or small family groups.

The large, wader-like Spotted Thick-Knee has prominent yellow eyes and long, yellow legs with three forward-pointing toes. It is active at night when it becomes very vocal and feeds on many invertebrates, small snakes, frogs and seeds.

COURSERS

Family: Glareolidae

Number of species: 3

Coursers are small, long-legged terrestrial birds with cryptic plumage. They are nomadic visitors to open areas suitable for foraging and breeding. They prefer the drier parts of southern Africa such as the Kgalagadi. Their food consists mainly of insects but they also eat seeds.

DOUBLE-BANDED COURSER ★

Dubbelbanddrawwertjie

Rhinoptilus africanus

Look for Double-banded Coursers in barren areas with little vegetation as a result of drought, veld fires or overgrazing. This bird is undoubtedly one of the best desert-adapted birds in the Kgalagadi. It does not need to drink water and can withstand extreme heat. The barren areas at Unions End is one of its favourite locations.

The mottled buff Double-banded Courser, with its long legs and two conspicuous bold and black bands on its chest, is indeed one of the star species of semi-deserts. It feeds mainly on harvester termites, and prefers to feed during dawn or dusk or even at night when the moon is bright. Irrespective of conditions, it breeds right through the year, laying one rather big egg at a time on the barren soil without any shade. When it becomes intensely hot, the breeding adult will stand up to protect the egg from the sun's lethal rays. The adults have a nest-relieve system in the full sun, allowing them to cool off for some time. The hatchling is well developed and receives the undivided attention of both parents. In this way, all the energy is invested in one individual at various periods of the year, thus improving the likelihood of the species' survival.

TEMMINCK'S COURSER ★

Trekdrawwertjie

Cursorius temminckii

Similar to Burchell's Coursers in appearance and behaviour; insectivorous but do also feed on seeds; prefer open areas; fairly common resident in the far north of the park.

BURCHELL'S COURSER

Bloukopdrawwertjie

Cursorius rufus

Similar to Temminck's Courser in appearance and behaviour; insectivorous but do also feed on seeds; uncommon nomad.

LAPWINGS AND PLOVERS

Family: Charadriidae

Number of species: 2

Lapwings and plovers are a vast family of small- to medium-sized birds. Lapwings are medium-sized terrestrial birds with long bare legs, short toes and short, straight bills. All species mainly eat insects. They are noisy and prefer open areas to forage. Most species prefer open and moist grassland or mudbanks so just a few species represent the family in the Kgalagadi. The Three-banded Plover is the only species from the plover group.

CROWNED LAPWING ★

Kroonkiewiet

Vanellus coronatus

The Crowned Lapwing is common and seen along dry riverbeds and on mudbanks next to waterholes, where it forages for insects, especially termites.

The Crowned Lapwing's red legs and white-ringed black crown are diagnostic features. Its noisiness attracts attention, especially during the breeding season. Watching these birds can be pretty entertaining, especially when they dive-bomb other animals when they have chicks.

BLACKSMITH LAPWING

Bontkiewiet

Vanellus armatus

Look for Blacksmith Lapwings close to water on the western extremities of the park.

The boldly pied, black and white Blacksmith Lapwing with its greyish back prefers open habitats close to the water and has a small distribution in the Kgalagadi. It forages on shorelines of water bodies such as pans and overflowing water from boreholes for small invertebrates. Its 'klink klink klink' call sounds like a hammer on an anvil, hence the name.

THREE-BANDED PLOVER

Driebandstrandkiewiet

Charadrius tricollaris

Three-banded Plovers are nomadic visitors that forage in shallow fresh water and muddy shorelines. These distinctve birds attract attention by their harsh screechy calls.

GUINEAFOWLS

Family: Numididae

Number of species: 1

Helmeted Guineafowls are the only birds of this family likely to be seen in the Kgalagadi. They are endemic to Africa but uncommon in arid areas.

HELMETED GUINEAFOWL

Gewone tarentaal

Numida meleagris

The Helmeted Guineafowl is nomadic and largely occurs in the far southeast, near human settlements where water is readily available.

The bony casque and blue and red wattles on the head are an unmistakable feature of this bird. They must drink daily and prefer to roost on elevated structures or big trees. As opportunists, they feed on bulbs like plant stems, grass seeds and even dubbeltjie seeds. During early summer they forage for termites and other insects, providing the females with protein for egg production.

BIRDS THAT HUNT INSECTS IN FLIGHT – AERIAL HUNTERS

The majority of small carnivorous birds are insect-eating (insectivorous). Most insectivorous birds obtain moisture from their prey and do not need to drink regularly.

NIGHTJARS

Family: Caprimulgidae
Number of species: 2

Nightjars are medium-sized nocturnal or crepuscular birds with long wings, short legs and short bills.

RUFOUS-CHEEKED NIGHTJAR

Rooiwangnaguil
Caprimulgus rufigena

▾ The Rufous-cheeked Nightjar is an intra-African breeding summer migrant. Look for it in wooded areas during dawn, dusk or later in the day on the wing.

The Rufous-cheeked Nightjar is similar to the Fiery-necked Nightjar but has a vague rufous collar. Both sexes have pale markings on the outer wings and at the tail corners, which are white in males and buff in females. This migratory species visits a variety of open habitats during migration and the non-breeding season.

FIERY-NECKED NIGHTJAR

Afrikaanse Naguil
Caprimulgus pectoralis

▴ Travellers on the 4x4 routes into Botswana may encounter these birds at dusk or dawn while on the hunt. Look for them in or near woodland areas.

The Fiery-necked Nightjar is medium-sized with a solid rufous collar. Both sexes have minor pale marks on the outer wings and large ones at the tail corners, which are white in males and buff in females. They occur in various habitats, including a small part of the arid savanna. Its song is a distinctive series of whistles: 'dear lord, deliver us!' It is similar to the Rufous-cheeked Nightjar but darker in colour with a brighter and more distinct rufous collar. Males have less white on the wing and more on the tail than the Rufous-cheeked Nightjar. Females have more prominent buff tail corners than Rufous-cheeked Nightjars.

SWIFTS

Family: Apodidae

Number of species: 4

The swift is a medium-sized aerial bird that is a superb flyer. Sleeping, eating, bathing and even mating on the wing, swifts rarely touch the ground. They are among the fastest birds in the world in level flight, with an impressive top speed of 111 km/h. They are superficially like swallows; however, they are not closely related to any passerine species.

Swifts are a darker brown than swallows, particularly on their bellies, so they will look black against the sky. They have proportionally longer narrow wings that resemble a boomerang and their forked tails are much shorter and stouter than the elongated pronged tail of a swallow. Swifts spend most of their time flying and they never perch.

AFRICAN PALM SWIFT

Palmwindswael

Cypsiurus parvus

The Palm Swift occurs only in the far south of the park.

This small swift is unmistakable with its uniform dark-grey colouring, pointed, slender wings and very long, deeply forked, thin tail. The eyes are brown and the bill, legs and feet are pinkish-grey.

RO

COMMON SWIFT

Europese Windswael

Apus apus

The Common Swift is a non-breeding summer visitor from Europe and occurs throughout the park.

The Common Swift has uniformly black plumage and a whitish throat but its tail is not as deeply forked as others.

RO

LITTLE SWIFT

Kleinwindswael

Apus affinis

RO

Little Swifts occur in various habitats, are resident and often seen in camps.

The Little Swift is recognisable by its broad white rump, square tail and white throat. Its wings are rounder rather than pointed, like those of other swifts. They occur in large flocks.

WHITE-RUMPED SWIFT

Witkruiswindswael

Apus caffer

This White-rumped Swift is a breeding migrant and is seen only in summer. Recognise it by the deeply forked tail, white crescent on the rump and whitish throat.

RO

SWALLOWS AND MARTINS

Family: Hirundinidae

Number of species: 3

Swallows and martins are primarily small, elegant, aerial species with long, tapered wings, forked tails (swallows have elongated outer feathers) and small bills, but wide mouths for catching insects in flight.

Swallows are the most colourful group, with most of them at least having some iridescent blue plumage, along with patches of russet or chestnut-rufous plumage, usually on the head, breast or belly. They have deeply forked tails, some of which have elongated outer rectrices commonly referred to as streamers.

The martins are dull, primarily brown and grey, resemble swallows but have broader, short and pointed wings. Their tails are slightly forked compared to the swallows and lack streamers.

ROCK MARTIN

Kransswael

Ptyonoprogne fuligula

Look for them in the park's camps or the hides beside waterholes. They prefer rocky outcrops and may be seen near the calcareous outcrops, where they attach their nests under the shelters of overhangs. They are reasonably common in the park.

RO

The distinguishing features of the Rock Martin are the grey-brown upper and pale buff underparts. The windows are visible when it spreads its square tail in flight. It is usually seen alone, in pairs or loose, small flocks. It flies slowly, glides, swerves and turns while it takes insects on the wing.

They have enduring pair bonds since they tend to return to their nests year after year.

BROWN-THROATED MARTIN

Afrikaanse Oewerswael

Riparia paludicola

Look for these birds where there is water and after plentiful rains. They occur in large flocks and are gregarious. They hawk small insect prey in flight, picking it from grass-tops or water surfaces.

RO

Brown-throated Martins are not as common as Rock Martins, but are similar. They also have dark grey-brown upperparts, heads, throats and breasts but can be distinguished by their white belly and underparts. The tail is slightly forked, the bill is black and the legs and feet are pinkish-brown.

BARN SWALLOW

Europese Swael

Hirundo rustica

You will find these birds only in summer since it is a common non-breeding migrant. It occurs in big flocks after summer rains in the region.

Recognise the Barn Swallow by its red-brown forehead and throat bordered by a broad, black band. The upperparts are glossy blue-black and it is whitish below. The tail is deeply forked with exceptionally long outer feathers. In flight, the white underwings and broad black edges are distinctive.

SMALLER BIRDS THAT HUNT FROM A PERCH

Many insectivorous and medium- to small-sized birds use a perch to spot potential prey. These include drongos, rollers, bee-eaters, flycatchers and some shrikes. These birds are conspicuous as they usually sit on an exposed vantage point and some attract attention by their brightly coloured plumage.

DRONGO

Family: Dicruridae
Number of species: 1

The drongos are a family of passerine birds but only one species occurs in the arid savanna of the Kgalagadi. Drongos are primarily black or dark grey, short-legged birds with an upright stance when perched. They have forked tails.

FORK-TAILED DRONGO ★

Mikstertbyvanger
Dicrurus adsimilis

The aggressive and bold Fork-tailed Drongo is a regular sighting in the Kgalagadi. Look for it near grazing antelope and the greener river valleys.

It feeds on various food items, including insects, scorpions and smaller vertebrates. Like raptors, it holds the prey in one foot while tearing it apart. The drongo is a very opportunistic bird that often accompanies grazing animals to catch insects they disturb. It also robs other birds of their prey. The seemingly fearless drongo frequently mobs raptors. This is a tactic used to encourage the raptor to leave the vicinity. The drongo recognises the raptor as a predatory threat but it is aware that the raptor relies on the element of surprise to attack prey. Being smaller and more manoeuvrable, the drongo can dive-bomb perched raptors or, on occasion, those in flight, pecking them behind the head without fear of being caught by the larger bird, which has neither surprise nor speed-from-rest to its advantage.

FLYCATCHERS

Family: Muscicapidae
Number of species: 4

Flycatchers are a massive family of primarily small- to medium-sized birds. They feed on insects caught in the air or ground, usually by hawking from a perch.

MARICO FLYCATCHER ★

Maricovlieëvanger

Melaeornis mariquensis

The Marico Flycatcher is one of the most common and conspicuous little brown birds. These birds are not easily disturbed and sometimes enter rest camps.

It is identified by its white underparts and contrasting brown upperparts. Marico Flycatchers are perch-and-pounce hunters using perches in the lower stratum of trees or shrubs. They catch and consume most of their insect prey on the ground.

CHAT FLYCATCHER

Grootvlieëvanger

Melaeornis infuscatus

The Chat Flycatcher is another cryptically coloured flycatcher favouring the northern areas of the park with more trees. Therefore, look out for it in the Nossob area. It is a common resident.

FISCAL FLYCATCHER

Fiskaalvlieëvanger

Melaenornis silens

The Fiscal Flycatcher is a resident but is seldom seen. Search for it in rest camps.

The species name silens comes from the Latin word 'silence' or 'resting', describing these birds' relatively quiet nature. The Fiscal Flycatcher gets its English and Afrikaans common names from its resemblance to the common fiscal, which in turn gets its name from its suit-and-tie appearance reminiscent of the taxman ('fiscal').

SPOTTED FLYCATCHER

Europese Vlieëvanger

Muscicapa striata

This non-breeding migrant comes from Eurasia and spends the summer in the far south of Africa where it is common in the Kgalagadi. Notice the slim build and very long wings, typical of a migratory bird. It is easily overlooked and occurs in any woodland on lowish perches from which it darts to catch insects in flight.

ROLLERS

Family: Coraciidae

Number of species: 3

These birds are known as rollers because of the aerial acrobatics they perform during courtship or territorial flights. Rollers share the colourful appearance of kingfishers and bee-eaters with blues and pinkish or cinnamon-browns predominating. The two inner front toes are connected, while the outer one isn't.

They are mainly insect eaters, diving from a perch to catch food from the ground. They are monogamous and nest in an unlined hole in a tree.

LILAC-BREASTED ROLLER ★

Gewone Troupant

Coracias caudatus

▾ The colourful Lilac-breasted Rollers are a resident species in the Kgalagadi, although they are less common than in other moister savanna areas. They are favour the north of the park beyond Nossob. They occur solitary or in pairs.

Their bright, spectacular plumage is best seen in flight. They have remarkable eyesight and spend much of the day hunting from a convenient perch, flying down to catch large insects and other prey on the ground.

PURPLE ROLLER

Groot Troupant

Coracias naevius

▴ Look for the Purple Roller in open woodland and savanna. They are occasionally seen in the northern and Botswana parts of the park.

This sturdy Purple Roller is recognised by its blue square tail, olive-green back, prominent white eyebrow and purple underparts with white stripes. Purple Rollers prefer thornveld and occur along the Auob and the Nossob riverbeds.

EUROPEAN ROLLER

Europese Troupant

Coracias garrulous

▸ Find them only in the far north. They are non-breeding summer visitor; uncommon in the Kgalagadi.

BEE-EATERS

Family: Meropidae

Number of species 2

Bee-eaters have pointed wings and long, manoeuvrable tails that allow fast and agile flight. As the name implies, these birds are insectivores and feed primarily on flying insects with stings like bees and wasps. Bee-eaters hunt using a technique called hawking, hunting on the wing for food, and they seldom come down onto the ground to hunt.

SWALLOW-TAILED BEE-EATER ★

Swaelstertbyevreter

Merops hirundineus

Look for the nests of Swallow-tailed Bee-eaters along the high earthen ridges of the roads (early summer). They excavate burrows themselves in suitable embankments, such as low sandbanks, even in surprisingly low sandbanks. Marie's Loop near Nossob is one of the favourite spots for breeding.

The Swallow-tailed Bee-eater is the only breeding resident bee-eater in the Kgalagadi and often perches in trees next to the road. Unlike most other bee-eater species, the Swallow-tailed Bee-eaters are not gregarious and occur singly or in small groups. During the cold, semi-desert winter nights, Swallow-tailed Bee-eaters huddle together on a branch for warmth. They catch insects in flight, primarily wasps and bees.

KINGFISHERS

Family: Alcedinidae

Number of species: 1

Six species of African kingfishers feed on insects, arachnids and small vertebrates, mostly captured after diving onto dry land. Only one of these non-fishing kingfishers is a resident of the Kgalagadi. Kingfishers are territorial and mark their territories by repeated calling and highly conspicuous displays of flaring and vibrating their wings.

STRIPED KINGFISHER

Gestreepte Visvanger

Halcyon chelicuti

Look for the Striped Kingfisher near waterholes. It is a resident but uncommon in the park.

The Striped Kingfisher belongs to the tree kingfisher subfamily. This bird is highly territorial and will ward off birds from its species and doves, rollers and shrikes. Their territory may be up to three hectares and hold 100 tall trees. It is surveyed from a treetop by its owner, which sings intermittently from before dawn until after midday.

The Striped Kingfisher feeds primarily on grasshoppers and other large insects. Small lizards, snakes and rodents are occasionally taken. It hunts from a high perch, swooping to the ground for prey up to 10 times a minute. Food items are taken back to the perch and swallowed. They beat large prey vigorously first before they ingest it.

EUROPEAN BEE-EATER

Europese Byevreter

Merops apiaster

Look out for the European Bee-eater only in summer since it is a non-breeding summer visitor mainly to the south of the park.

The European Bee-eater is the most colourful bee-eater with a yellow throat, narrow black collar and a brown/chestnut and yellow back. It is a non-breeding summer visitor in the south of the park.

SHRIKES

Family: Laniidae

Number of species: 5

The term 'shrike' includes true, helmet, and bush-shrikes; a well-known group of small- to medium-sized birds with strong, hooked, toothed, raptor-like bills. As skilled insect hunters, they have eked out a living in the arid savanna. They don't need to drink because their prey supplies enough moisture for them to survive. Bush-shrikes are not exclusively perch hunters but find their food mainly in and around trees and shrubs.

RED-BACKED SHRIKE ★

Rooiruglaksman

Lanius collurio

In this small shrike the male is distinctive, with a blue-grey head, black mask and rusty-brown back. The female has warm brown upperparts and fine dark scalloping on her breast and flanks. It is a common migrant in summer but is non-breeding.

Look for these birds in open areas with scattered bushes and trees. They especially favour areas with thorny plants. The shrike impales prey (small birds, large insects, rodents) to create 'larders'. It hunts from perches on top of bushes but is also retiring and easily overlooked at other times.

SOUTHERN OR COMMON FISCAL SHRIKE ★

Fiskaallaksman

Lanius collaris

Look for Fiscal Shrikes perched on trees along the road, hunting for insects. They are easy to recognise. You will often find them near grazing antelope or the foraging honey badgers waiting for insects that are disturbed.

The common fiscal is a widespread bird. The white 'V' on the black back and all white underparts are distinctive features but the western race occurring in the Kgalagadi has a white eyebrow. It feeds mainly on insects, although spiders and small vertebrates form part of its diet. The Fiscal Shrike is also known as 'Jacky Hangman' because it sometimes skewers insect prey on a sharp thorn.

LESSER GREY SHRIKE ★

Gryslaksman

Lanius minor

▲ **Look out for this species from late November to December until they depart in the first 10 days of April.**

The Lesser Grey Shrike is a specialist of acacia thornveld in the Kalahari basin and has a distribution similar to other thornveld specialists. It does not need to drink and prefers open, arid places with low and tall trees alternating with open grassy spaces. It is a non-breeding, endemic migrant. The Kalahari basin is a favourite destination.

SOUTHERN WHITE-CROWNED SHRIKE

Kremetartlaksman

Eurocephalus anguitimens

▼ **Look for the White-crowned Shrike in the southern parts of the park, particularly along the Auob River. It perches and watches for invertebrates, which it hawks off trunks or hunts on the ground before returning to a sentinel perch.**

The White-crowned Shrike is a bulky, large-headed vanilla-and-brown shrike. It is a resident and occurs singly or in small groups of up to six. It prefers to perch conspicuously on taller trees adjacent to bare ground.

SMALLER BIRDS THAT FORAGE IN AND AROUND TREES AND SHRUBS

Most tree-living (arboreal) birds feed on smaller prey such as insects, spiders, worms and smaller vertebrates. They forage in trees and shrubs or on the ground. These birds are not easily seen or photographed as they are constantly on the move. This group includes the bush-shrikes, scrub robins, thrushes, chats and robins, hoopoes, scimitarbills and wood hoopoes, woodpeckers, cuckoos, tits, babblers, warblers, crombecs, eremomelas, cisticolas, prinias and warblers.

CRIMSON-BREASTED SHRIKE ★

Rooiborslaksman

Laniarius atrococcineus

The rest camps are the best place to watch the conspicuous and iconic Crimson-breasted Shrikes. On your game drive you will find them along the dry riverbeds. Males and females look alike.

The Crimson-breasted Shrike is striking with its black upperparts with white stripes and bright-red underparts. It belongs to the group of true shrikes but differs from the others in that it does not usually hunt from a perch. This Kgalagadi special is an insect feeder with a preference for ants they catch on the ground or in the bark of trees. These breathtakingly beautiful birds with their evocative duet, create the impression of a wonder world in the Kgalagadi Desert.

BUSH-SHRIKES

Family: Malaconotidae

Number of species: 3

The bush-shrikes are smallish passerine birds. They were formerly grouped with the true shrikes in the family Laniidae. They are now considered sufficiently distinctive to be separated from that group as the family Malaconotidae, a name that alludes to their fluffy back and rump feathers.

BRUBRU

Bontroklaksman

Nilaus afer

The Brubru shrike is more often heard than seen. The species' distinctive main call is remarkably telephone-like, a ringing burry 'preeeeee' with some associated clicks and whistles. They are fairly common and occur solitary or in pairs.

The Brubru is a small, primarily black and white bush-shrike with a pale wing stripe and a chequered back. A solid chestnut stripe runs from the shoulders to the flanks in most races, but in some races it is absent. Females have fewer bold marks than males. Pairs frequently join mixed-species flocks in arid savanna and broadleaf woodland, where they acrobatically glean for invertebrates.

BOKMAKIERIE

Bokmakierie

Telophorus zeylonus

Look for this striking bird in open habitats with camelthorns to perch.

The Bokmakierie is closely related to the true shrike. Unlike the true shrikes that perch conspicuously in the open, the Bokmakierie is shy and skulking. This bird has a typical shrike diet of insects, small lizards, snakes, small birds and frogs.

The Bokmakierie has a range of loud whistles and calls, sometimes in duet.

BROWN-CROWNED TCHAGRA

Rooivlerktjagra

Tchagra australis

Brown-crowned pairs skulk near the ground where they hop and glean for insects in scrub, tangled thickets and open woodland. The species is more terrestrial than other tchagras.

This bush-shrike has rufous wings, a bold pale eyebrow and a diagnostic brown central crown bordered by black stripes. It performs a descending spiral aerial display while making a 'prrrrrp' rattle sound with its fluttering wings before singing a rapid descending series of 15–20 musical 'chee-ree' notes as the bird returns to the ground.

PRIRIT BATIS

Priritbosbontrokkie

Batis pririt

Look for the Pririt Batis in dry thornveld and dense bushes around waterholes. It is a common resident and occurs in pairs or family groups. Look for it low in the bushes where it usually forages.

The Pririt Batis, also known as the Pririt Puff-back Flycatcher or Pririt Puffback, is a small passerine bird in the wattle-eye family. It is a resident of southern Africa and southwestern Angola. It is a small, stout insect-eating bird in dry, broadleaf woodland and thorn scrub.

♀

TITS

Family: Paridae

Number of species: 1

Tits are small birds with plain or colourful plumages, stout legs, strong feet and short, triangular bills. They are social and gather in mixed flocks but territorial when nesting.

ASHY TIT ★

Acaciagrysmees

Parus cinerascens

The Ashy Tit is a resident that forages along dry riverbeds where there is scrubby vegetation. It is also found in the rest camps.

The Ashy Tit is a large greyish tit with a black-and-white head pattern and a black bib. Pairs and small groups favour arid savanna and thorn trees, foraging for insects in small groups or mixed-species flocks. Their song is typically a series of short, repeated musical notes – 'treeuw-treeuw-treeuw-treeuw' – with chattering, trills or dry buzzing interspersed.

PENDULINE-TITS

Family: Remizidae

Number of species: 1

Small, somewhat gregarious birds with the nest a hanging purse of densely felted plant or animal fibres with close-able tubular entrance. Below this is a ledge on which the bird perches to open entrance tube that forms a false entrance.

CAPE PENDULINE-TIT

Kaapse Kapokvoël

Remiz minutus

The Penduline-tit is not easy to find. It prefers taller camelthorns for nesting while they forage in groups, often in low bushes. The tit can also be detected by its song, a repeated series of 5–7 high-pitched 'chiueew' notes. Multiple birds may also give simple high-pitched tinkling and rasping notes.

The Penduline-tit is among the smallest birds in southern Africa. It is a tiny, short-tailed bird with a small thin bill, yellowish underparts, a green back and a grey head with delicate grizzled black-and-white scaly patterning on the forehead. Pairs and small groups forage restlessly for invertebrates and fruits, dangling upside down while they search.

This bird has developed a clever way to protect its nest to withstand the forceful Kalahari winds. The wind may throw the pendulous nest back and forth; sometimes it is thrown almost upside down but it remains safe and protected. The parents use sticky spiderwebs to attach it to the thin branch holding the nest firmly in place. A unique feature is the crafty construction of the nest to protect the adult birds, eggs and chicks by leading potential enemies to a false entrance. On one side above the pouch-shaped almost solid lower part of the nest, there is a notch with a 'roof' over it, which looks like an entrance. But it does not lead into the nest – only into a small empty chamber. The actual entrance is right on top of the false one. The 'roof' is a trapdoor that closes as soon as a tit has entered or left the nest. It Is near-endemic.

Gerda van Schalkwyk

SCRUB ROBINS, THRUSHES, CHATS AND WHEATEARS

Family Muscicapidae
Number of species: 6

SCRUB ROBINS

Scrub robins, or bush chats, are medium-sized insectivorous birds. They are primarily African species that inhabit open woodland or scrub. These birds feed mainly on insects and nest on the ground or in bushes.

KALAHARI SCRUB ROBIN ★

Kalahariwipstert

Cercotrichas paena

Find this resident alone or in pairs hopping about, jerking its tail upwards and flicking its wings from time to time as it forages on the ground under three-thorn shrubs and other low bushes. The Kalahari Scrub Robin is a typical Kgalagadi bird favouring open sandveld and low bushes. Its morning song delights and the male is an excellent mimic.

THRUSHES

The thrushes are a passerine bird family with a worldwide distribution. They are small- to medium-sized ground-living birds that feed on insects, other invertebrates and fruit. Generally, thrushes are slender-billed songbirds with the lower leg 'booted'; covered in front with a single long scale instead of many short ones. The young have a spotted plumage at first with a single annual moult.

GROUNDSCRAPER THRUSH

Gevlekte Lyster

Turdus litsitsirupa

▾ Find the Groundscraper Thrush on bare patches or short grassy areas along the Auob and Nossob. It is a resident but is uncommon.

This thrush is heavily spotted on its white underparts and has a robust marked face. Pairs and small groups occupy grassland and open woodland, favouring heavily grazed and burnt areas. It can run long distances on the ground hunting invertebrates, stopping bolt upright and flicking its wings. It mainly eats insects, plucking them from the ground with short grass tufts, scratching and scraping in leaf litter. It occasionally forages aerially, taking insects flushed by bushfires.

SHORT-TOED ROCK THRUSH

Korttoonkliplyster

Monticola brevipes

▴ Look out for the Short-toed Rock Thrush on the rocky or calcareous outcrops, but it does prefer flat country in winter.

This rock thrush is similar to the Cape Rock Thrush but occurs in the arid savanna where it is nearly endemic. It is an altitudinal migrant with seasonal movements away from its breeding grounds.

CHATS

Chats are closely related to wheatears, allied to robins and flycatchers and more distantly related to thrushes. They prefer drier habitats, feeding on the ground, hopping along and gleaning from ground vegetation. They are not gregarious but sometimes occur in family groups. They feed on insects – mainly ants, termites and beetles – but will also take spiders and small reptiles.

FAMILIAR CHAT ★

Gewone Spekvreter

Oenanthe familiaris

▲ Look for the Familiar Chat in the rest camps where it becomes habituated to the presence of people.

The Familiar Chat is a plain grey-brown bird with rusty ear patches, a rufous rump and black-tipped outer tail feathers. It tends to be slightly smaller in the Kgalagadi than in mesic areas. The juvenile is buffy-spotted above and scaled blackish below. It often perches conspicuously and then drops to the ground or into a bush to feed on invertebrates. It frequently flicks both wings simultaneously and lifts its tail. It hops on the ground and flicks its tail with every stop, foraging for insects and animal fat.

ANT-EATING CHAT ★

Swartpiek

Myrmecocichla formicivore

▼ Look for the Ant-eating Chat in areas with scrubby vegetation and termite mounds, especially north of Dikbaardskolk.

This endemic chat looks plain brown or black from a distance but shows a faint reddish-brown mottling close up. Common and conspicuous, it often perches upright on termite mounds, rocks or bushes. This chat is unusual in that it nests and roosts in the roof of a hole in the ground occupied by brown hyena and aardvark. Only the female incubates the eggs. However, these chats are targeted by the Greater Honeyguide, a brood parasite.

WHEATEARS

Wheatears are closely related to chats. Of the five local species, just one occurs in the Kgalagadi. These species are recognisable by their conspicuous white rump and white-edged tails, which terminate in a black bar as an inverted T. Male wheatears are strikingly coloured but the females are rather bland.

CAPPED WHEATEAR ★

Hoëveldskaapwagter

Oenanthe pileata

Look for the Capped Wheatear in open areas. It stands boldly upright on low perches such as rocks or dung piles from where it forages. It is unusual in that it nests in ground cavities made by rodents.

This boldly patterned Capped Wheatear prefers arid areas or even burnt veld in search of dead or fleeing insects, ants and other invertebrates. It forages on the ground and captures its prey using a dash-and-jab technique. It uses low perches such as rocks or dung piles to sing and scan for predators.

Distinguishing features are the white eyebrow, black mask through the eye and black band across the chest. The outer half of the tail is black and the inner half is white, which is conspicuous in flight. It often spreads its tail, bows, bobs its head or flicks its wings.

HOOPOES

Family: Upupidae

Number of species: 1

There are three living hoopoe species worldwide, but only one occurs in Africa. All have a long, slightly decurved bill and fan-like crest. The broad, rounded wings and square-ended tail are black and white.

AFRICAN HOOPOE

Hoephoep

Upupa Africana

Look for hoopoes in the riverbeds around trees and other vegetation, probing for food in the ground.

Hoopoes are medium-sized birds. Their most distinctive feature is the conspicuous fan-like erectile crest with broad black tips. They are good runners, using their long, pointed and decurved bills to probe into the soil. There they forage on the ground for insects, worms and small lizards. They detect food by sight, touch and smell and use leaf-tossing. They do not probe bark, despite spending much time in trees, where they roost and make nests in tree cavities or rock crevices.

They can be spotted in pairs because they are monogamous when breeding. Courtship-feeding does occur. When nesting, they are strongly territorial. This species has an exciting predator avoidance strategy. The nestling and the breeding female has an enlarged preening gland that secretes a foul-smelling oil. This, and poor nest hygiene, results in a nest and nestlings that smell abominable.

SCIMITARBILLS

Family: Rhinopomastidae
Number of species: 1

Ornithologists used to classify scimitarbills in the wood hoopoe family, but the latest genetic studies show they diverged from the true wood hoopoes about 10 million years ago. Only one species belongs to this family, which also occurs in the Kgalagadi. It is endemic to Africa south of the Sahara.

COMMON SCIMITARBILL

Swartbekkakelaar

Rhinopomastus cyanomelas

Look for this species in the dry, thornveld savanna in the northern parts of the park. It feeds almost exclusively on invertebrates, running up and down tree trunks and branches, probing the bark with its bill while using its tail to stabilise itself. When foraging, it is usually solitary or in pairs, often hanging upside down.

The males and females look alike but the female has a shorter, robust bill to avoid feeding in the same area as the male. The males tend to feed on the trunk, starting near the bottom and working their way up, while the females forage on lesser branches near the canopy. They are monogamous and nest in tree holes. Only the female does the incubation, while the male feeds her. The greater honeyguide, a brood parasite, targets this species.

WOOD HOOPOES

Family: Phoeniculidae

Number of species: 1

Wood hoopoes are a small endemic family to Africa. The birds are dark, sleek, glossy and occur in the savanna or scrubland. Two species occur in southern Africa but only the Green Wood-hoopoe occurs in the Kgalagadi.

GREEN WOOD-HOOPOE

Rooibekkakelaar

Phoeniculus purpureus

Look for small, noisy groups of Green Wood-hoopoes in the river valleys lined with large camelthorns where they forage by climbing about in trees, probing with their bills in loose bark. They are mainly found around and north of Nossob.

Green Wood-hoopoes are small- to medium-sized birds with long, slender, decurved, slightly bent, red bills. Their plumage is mainly black with glossy green or purple undertones. The wings are broad, rounded and long. The tail feathers are graduated and divided into steps of different lengths, with white spots on the tips. The long toes, short red legs and hooked claws enable them to climb about in trees looking for insects, lizards and millipedes.

They move around in small, noisy groups, with only one breeding pair, which means they are cooperative breeders. Together, they defend their territory to keep intruders and predators away, and the helpers assist in feeding the young. Like the Scimitarbill, the males and females look alike, but the female has a shorter and less decurved bill that helps to rule out competition for food since they forage on different parts of a tree. They also have a strong-smelling preening gland that produces a vulgar smell and is off-putting for predators. The greater honeyguide, a brood parasite, targets this species.

WOODPECKERS

Family: Picidae

Number of species: 2

Woodpeckers have long, straight, powerful beaks for chiselling and drilling into wood. Because of the wear and tear involved, the beak grows continuously to replace keratin that flakes away. The base of the bill is broad and acts as a shock absorber. The neck muscles of a woodpecker are well developed to power the drilling strokes of the neck and head.

A woodpecker's skull is sturdy enough to absorb the blows of hammering wood. A unique hinge between the nasal and frontal bones dissipates the shock, and the delicate brain is cushioned within the skull to counter these effects.

The woodpeckers have another foraging strategy: they obtain insects by probing their bills in cracks and holes and sometimes extracting grubs using their long, barbed tongue. Their feet are adapted for clinging to the vertical trunks of trees.

CARDINAL WOODPECKER

Kardinaalspeg

Dendropicos fuscescens

Look for them on dead tree branches or follow its angry-sounding, dry, trilled rattle call that gives it away.

The Cardinal Woodpecker is the most common species in the Kgalagadi and southern Africa. It is a small, compact woodpecker with heavily streaked underparts and a solid black moustachial streak. The top of the female's head is dark, the male's forecrown is brown and the hind crown and nape are red.

GOLDEN-TAILED WOODPECKER

Goudstertspeg

Campethera abingoni

The Golden-tailed Woodpecker occurs only in the far north of the park and beyond into Botswana. It is uncommon elsewhere.

The Golden-tailed Woodpecker usually forages in trees, tapping and probing branches, looking for insects and licking them with its barbed tongue. It may also excavate insect nests and glean ants from branches. The thickened and rigid tail feather shaft, which is golden brown, helps to support the woodpecker while clinging to the side of a tree.

Both sexes excavate the nest, which is usually a hole in the underside of a tree branch. Here they lay their eggs, which are incubated by both sexes. The chicks are cared for by both parents. The adults store food in the crop for regurgitating to the chicks.

CUCKOOS

Family: Cuculidae

Number of species: 5

The cuckoo family is extensive and most are brood parasites, meaning they lay their eggs in other birds' nests. Thinking the egg is its own, the host incubates it and cares for the chick.

The true cuckoos are all intra-African migrants that visit southern Africa in summer. At the peak of the breeding season, their loud, continuous and repetitive calls are typical of the African bush in summer. Only the males call and it is thought that the intensity of their calls activates hormone development in the females to synchronise their egg laying with the host birds. Cuckoos are insectivorous and eat hairy caterpillars that most other birds avoid.

BLACK CUCKOO

Swart Koekoek

Cuculus clamosus

This cuckoo is uncommon migrant in the Kgalagadi but has been recorded in the south of the park. Like the other cuckoos, it is secretive and more often heard rather than seen.

It parasitises the Crimson-breasted Shrike and is found along the dry riverbeds. It is solitary and a summer migrant.

Rudolph Oosthuizen

AFRICAN CUCKOO

Afrikaanse Koekoek

Cuculus gularis

Expect to see the African Cuckoo from late August until March-April. Find them in the vicinity of Fork-tailed Drongos.

The African Cuckoo is highly elusive, perches just below the canopy of trees and therefore is easy to overlook. Males can be detected by their 'cuc-cuck' call from where they watch their surroundings. These parasitic birds are host-specific and parasitise Fork-tailed Drongos. It is well known that drongos are highly aggressive and it must therefore be quite a feat for them to lay their eggs in the drongos' nest. While the male distracts the drongos, the female slips into the nest and quickly lays her egg and removes one of the drongo eggs. The young cuckoo instinctively pushes the drongos' eggs out of the nest and then enjoys the undivided attention of the hosts.

GREAT SPOTTED CUCKOO

Gevlekte Koekoek

Clamator glandarius

Look for the Great Spotted Cuckoo in summer because it's a breeding migrant that parasites crows and starlings. It is conspicuous and noisy and spends most of its time in treetops.

This cuckoo is quite a large cuckoo in comparison to the others. The long tail, distinct pale grey chest and creamy white breast and throat are characteristic. The upperparts are dark grey with white spots. It is rowdy but more visible than other cuckoos as it forages lower down on trees. The hosts of this brood parasite are crows and some starling species.

DIEDERIK CUCKOO

Diederikkie

Chrysococcyx caprius

Look for the Diederik Cuckoo on camelthorns during the summer months. You will probably find them near their host species, which includes robins, sparrows and weavers.

The small glossy-green Diederik Cuckoo is a widespread member of the cuckoo family. Like other cuckoos, it is an intra-African breeding migrant that arrives in early summer, and soon the shrill 'dee-dee-deederic' call of the male can be heard almost everywhere. Like other cuckoos, the Diederik Cuckoo is a brood parasite but it has taken this extraordinary breeding strategy to an uncanny level of sophistication.

The cuckoo has a small build and is greenish in colour. The male has barred flanks, white flecking on the wing, white patches in front of and behind the eye, and a distinctly red eye surrounded by a red ring. The bronzy-green female has a diagnostic white patch in front of the eye, a plain back and white patches in the wings.

Unlike most other brood parasites, it has a wide range of hosts but the top hosts are common birds, such as the Southern Masked Weaver, Sociable Weaver and Cape Sparrow. What is most remarkable is that the eggs match those of the host. When the female lays her egg, she eats or ejects other eggs. The cuckoo's egg has a short incubation period and should there still be the hosts' chick, the cuckoo chick will evict them and receive the undivided attention of the hosts.

Diederiks feed mainly on caterpillars.

JACOBIN CUCKOO

Bontnuwejaarsvoël

Clamator jacobinus

Very uncommon.

The usually solitary Jacobin Cuckoo is a breeding migrant that visits in summer. It looks striking with its black-and-white plumage and conspicuous crest. The white wing bar is present in all races. Some birds exhibit a dark morph – all black with a white wing patch. Its song is a widely spaced series of somewhat hoarse whistled notes. It lays its eggs in the nests of babblers, bulbuls and shrikes.

TIT-BABBLERS, BABBLERS, CROMBECS AND EREMOMELAS

Family: Sylviidae

Number of species: 4

The tit-babblers, babblers and the crombecs were previously not regarded as part of the same family, but are now placed together in the same family.

Tit-babblers, babblers, crombecks, and eremomelas are all members of the diverse and ecologically important family of birds known as Old World babblers, sharing common traits that have enabled them to thrive in a variety of habitats worldwide. They are adaptable birds, capable of thriving in diverse environments across their range. They forage on the ground or in low vegetation, using their sharp bills to probe for prey and their agile movements to capture insects. They are known for their highly social behaviour, often forming tight-knit family groups or flocks.

TIT-BABBLERS

The name of this group can be attributed to their appearance. While the bird has a tit shape, it has plumage like the babbler. They have a rapid, undulating flight pattern. Usually alone or in pairs, they feed on insects and fruit and are strongly associated with acacia trees and dense undergrowth.

CHESTNUT-VENTED TIT-BABBLER (WARBLER) ★

Bosveldtjeriktiktik

Curruca subcoerulea

Look for it feeding on insects in camelthorns or dense undergrowth. It is usually alone or in pairs while gleaning low-down from leaves, stems and branches. It may also hawk insects in flight. It is monogamous and breeds opportunistically after rains. It is near-endemic.

The Chestnut-vented Tit-babbler (Warbler) is a common and confident little bird, usually seen singly or in pairs. This widespread warbler has different names and the Afrikaans name tjeriktiktik aptly mimics parts of its melodious and cheerful song.

It is an agile forager, rapidly moving through foliage in search of prey and occasionally hawking termite alates. It mainly feeds on insects gleaned from branches, supplemented with fruit.

The nest is a thin-walled cup of dry grass, rootlets and strips of bark secured with a spiderweb. It is typically placed in the branches of a bush or small tree. The Diederik and Jacobin Cuckoo sometimes parasitize their nests.

BABBLERS

There are five local babbler species but only the Southern Pied Babbler occurs in the Kgalagadi. They are sociable, living in co-operative breeding groups dominated by an alpha pair and they roost communally.

The birds forage largely on the ground in leaf litter within thickets. They feed on vertebrates, invertebrates and, on occasion, fruit.

SOUTHERN PIED BABBLER

Witkatlagter

Turdoides bicolor

Expect to see them in the far north or the Botswana section of the Kgalagadi.

The striking black-and-white babbler is endemic in southern Africa. Although it is a resident of an arid savanna, it is uncommon in the more open habitats of the Kgalagadi. Babblers are generally social birds and move around in family groups of 3–15. They prefer areas with thorn trees, such as the camelthorns, where they associate with Red-billed Buffalo Weavers. The species gives a high-pitched, aggravated babbling in the group chorus and gives an alarm when danger is suspected. They have an informal sentry where a group member perches in an elevated position to detect potential danger.

CROMBECS

Crombecs are unmistakable, with a short tail and relatively long, slender, slightly decurved bill. They forage by gleaning from twigs and leaves in the canopy of trees. Their strong legs enable them to hang upside down when foraging in bark cracks.

EREMOMELAS

Four local species exist but only the Yellow-bellied Eremomela occurs in the Kgalagadi. Here they are nomads responding to the conditions. They glean insects from twigs and leaves in the canopies of trees and occasionally hawk from a perch.

LONG-BILLED CROMBEC

Bosveldstompstert

Sylvietta rufescens

Find it clambering on bark and twigs searching for invertebrates and sporadically eating plant matter. It usually starts from the bottom, working its way up before flying to the next bush.

The Long-billed Crombec is a tiny, plump, almost tailless warbler with buff-orange underparts, grey-brown upperparts and a dark eye stripe that forms a buffy eyebrow.

It is often detected by its quiet but distinctive, faltering, ratchet-like song.

YELLOW-BELLIED EREMOMELA

Geelpensbossanger

Eremomela icteropygialis

Look for these small grey-brown birds with yellow belly, pale eyebrows and a dark eye stripe in scrubs and bushes. They thoroughly work through a bush before flitting to the next one. Fairly common.

PRINIAS, CISTICOLAS AND WARBLERS

Family: Cisticolidae

Number of species: 6

This family includes many small passerines, some formerly included in the Silviidae family. These small songbirds are the hardest of all birds to identify. They are dull grey to brown in colour, quick-moving and found in grasslands, scrublands and deserts. In the mornings, they may be seen sunbathing atop grasses or bushes.

Their drab plumage serves as a good camouflage. The crown and wing are often rufous coloured.

They have thin, straight bills adapted for gleaning insects and small invertebrates from foliage. Some hawk prey aerially. They usually don't flock, are secretive and drop away from sight. Most species are territorial and monogamous.

BLACK-CHESTED PRINIA ★

Swartbandlangstertjie

Prinia flavicans

The Black-chested Prinia is widespread and common in the dry savanna. It is inquisitive and perches conspicuously when disturbed.

Prinias are tiny warblers that can be distinguished from others by their long tails, frequently held in a near-vertical position. This prinia is the only species that has different breeding and non-breeding plumages. The Black-chested Prinia is aptly named for the charcoal-coloured breast band apparent in its breeding plumage.

DESERT CISTICOLA

Woestynklopkloppie

Cisticola aridulus

RO

Look for it in dry grasslands, including open stretches within savannas as they feed on insects.

The Desert Cisticola is widespread in the arid savanna. It is small, pale brown and heavily streaked. During breeding the plumage is darker but becomes washed out when not breeding.

Its song is a mix of high-pitched peeps, scratchy lower notes and 'tic' notes. It is highly similar to a Zitting Cisticola and can best be distinguished by song. However, subtle differences in plumage are present with the tail more uniformly dark and the rump slightly streaked.

ZITTING CISTICOLA

Landeryklopkloppie

Cisticola juncidis

Zitting Cisticolas are usually found in open grasslands where they hunt insects. Their repetitive and monotonous song, which is given from either a perch or an undulating song flight, is most readily detected.

This cisticola is an exceptionally widely distributed, small bird found mainly in grasslands. It is best identified by its rufous rump. It lacks gold on the collar and its rounded brownish tail has conspicuous spots. During the breeding season, males have a zigzagging flight display accompanied by regular 'zitting' calls that have been likened to repeated snips of a scissor. They build their pouch nest suspended within a clump of grass. Breeding males have a dark bill and crown.

RO

RUFOUS-EARED WARBLER

Rooioorlangstertjie

Malcorus pectoralis

EL

The Rufous-eared Warbler is a common resident that prefers low, shrubby vegetation on plains and dry watercourses. It resembles a prinia but its tail is even longer and wispier and usually lifted over its back. It is secretive and perches on bushes, and it is partly terrestrial, hopping or running rapidly between bushes. There is sexual colour dimorphism, which means males and females don't look alike. The Rufous-eared Warbler is endemic to southern Africa.

BARRED WREN-WARBLER

Gebande Sanger

Calamonastes fasciolatus

Rudolph Oosthuizen

Look for the Barred Wren-Warbler, which is an uncommon resident but has been recorded in the Mata Mata area of the park.

It is a long-tailed brownish warbler with heavy barring below. In breeding males, this barring is obscured by a brown band across the breast. It is generally uncommon in arid, thorny savanna and regularly raises its tail in a wren-like fashion. Its normal song is a vibrating, metallic note that is frequently repeated. It generally feeds on insects lower down in vegetation and is solitary or in pairs. It is near-endemic.

WILLOW WARBLER

Hofsanger

Phylloscopus trochilus

RO

This warbler is an uncommon non-breeding visitor to the Kgalagadi. It is small and difficult to identify but its sweet descending song assists in locating it.

WAGTAILS AND PIPITS

Family: Motacillidae

Number of species: 2

Wagtails and pipits belong to this family. They are small passerines with long, slender bodies, thin, pointed bills and medium to long tails. Pipits are usually a streaked or mottled brown. Longclaws are absent from the Kgalagadi. Wagtails and pipits are ground dwellers and eat insects, spiders and some plant matter. Wagtails get their name from the way they wag their tails up and down.

WAGTAILS

The wagtail bills are long and slender, adapted to gleaning. The long tail may help with balancing when foraging on the ground. They walk rather than hop while constantly wagging their tails up and down. They are often seen close to water and enter it to cool off. They are monogamous and territorial.

CAPE WAGTAIL

Gewone Kwikkie

Motacilla capensis

They are usually seen bobbing along the short grasses in the middle of the dry riverbeds of the Kgalagadi.

Cape Wagtails can be distinguished from other wagtail species by their broad breast band, brownish upperparts and buffy-white underparts. With its distinctive tireless wagging tail there is no mistaking the Cape Wagtail, regardless of its rather dull coloration. It is usually solitary or in pairs, foraging for insects on the ground.

PIPITS

These birds can easily be confused with larks but are generally larger and have a more horizontal stance. When not breeding, they are usually gregarious. Being terrestrial they are cryptically coloured and crouch rather than fly when disturbed. When they fly, it is to a perch where the origin of the disturbance can be seen. They dust-bathe and will also bathe in puddles of water. They are almost exclusively insectivorous and find all their food on the ground.

AFRICAN PIPIT

Gewone Koester

Anthus cinnamomeus

They are frequently seen bobbing along the short grasses in the middle of the dry riverbeds of the Kgalagadi.

The African Pipit is brown above and pale below, with a streaked back, well-marked face and white outer tail feathers. There is considerable geographic variation, from pale and sandy to rich brown and rufous. It is similar to other pipits and some key features to look for include the yellow base of the bill, streaked back and white outer tail feathers.

BUFFY PIPIT

Vaalkoester

Anthus vaalensis

Find the Buffy Pipit in open areas with short grass and along road verges where it forages insects on the ground. It is also a local migrant.

This is a large pipit with buffy outer tail feathers and a plain or very diffusely streaked back. It runs or walks but stops often, standing boldly upright, puffing out its breast and wagging its tail. It wags its tail more frequently and vigorously than other pipits.

OMNIVOROUS BIRDS

Omnivorous birds make up a considerable percentage of resident birds. Because of their diverse diets, they can survive periods of drought. These include hornbills, bulbuls, starlings, crows, chats, barbets and lovebirds.

HORNBILLS

Family: Bucerotidae
Number of species: 2

These medium to giant birds have huge decurved bills, often brightly coloured. There are two species in the Kgalagadi.

Hornbills have a remarkable nesting strategy. They are territorial and have only one mate per season. During the breeding season (September to March), the male advertises his territory from a conspicuous perch by raising his wings above his back to reveal the eye-catching black and white feathered pattern and bill pointing downwards towards his feet. Sometimes, the female will join him. They use suitable holes in trees to breed but before the process gets underway, the male will engage in courtship feeding to ensure the female is in prime condition before she starts breeding. Once inside the hole, she will seal the entrance with dung and mud provided by the male, leaving only a narrow slit. From then onwards, she gets the male's undivided attention, which keeps feeding her. She lays eggs, drops her feathers and becomes very fat. Once the eggs hatch, she stops eating and, during this period, she utilises the reserve fat stored in her body and starts growing feathers. The male keeps on providing food for the chicks.

When the female is of standard size and has grown feathers again, she breaks out of the nest. The chicks immediately start closing the opening from the inside, using their droppings. Both parents are then available to feed the growing chicks until they are nearly fully grown and are ready to break open the entrance to leave the nest. The adults continue feeding the chicks for another three weeks.

AFRICAN GREY HORNBILL

Grysneushoringvoël

Lophocerus nasutus

It forages in trees and hawks insects in flight. When calling, it flaps its wings and points its bill upwards. It is also omnivorous.

SOUTHERN YELLOW-BILLED HORNBILL

Geelbekneushoringvoël

Tockus leucomelas

Yellow-billed Hornbills mainly occur where camelthorns are abundant but they are not as common as in wetter savanna regions.

These hornbills are arboreal and widespread in acacia savanna areas of Africa. Climate change threatens their survival in the park. They eat insects but also some smaller vertebrates, fruit and seeds.

BULBULS

Family Pycnonotidae
Number of species: 1

These are small- to medium-sized arboreal birds that feed on fruits, insects and nectar. Bulbuls are important dispersal agents for fruiting plants and are instrumental in pollinating many flowers as they probe for nectar. All have small, dark, erectile crests and yellow vents. They all have a bare patch of skin around the eyes, the colour of which differs in each species. Only one species occurs in the Kgalagadi.

AFRICAN RED-EYED BULBUL ★

Rooioogtiptol

Pycnonotus nigricans

The African Red-eyed Bulbul is common in the Kgalagadi and has remarkable habitat tolerance. You will see this bird in the rest camps and along the riverbeds.

In the Kgalagadi, it prefers drainage lines with trees, where it feeds on insects and softer parts of plants. The fleshy red ring around the eyes identifies it. This bird is a near-endemic.

Look for them where they may be foraging in trees for fruit or hawking and gleaning insects and other vertebrates. They form long-term pair bonds and often allopreen each other. The Jacobin Cuckoo, a brood parasite, targets them to raise their young.

CROWS

Family: Corvidae

Number of species: 2

Crows are regarded as some of the most intelligent of all birds. They are large with heavy bills and nostrils covered in bristles. They are all omnivorous and also scavenge. Ground feeders, principally, take a variety of invertebrates, vertebrates and plant material. They may walk into the water to bathe. All species are territorial and monogamous (have only one partner) and make raptor-like stick platform nests. The Great Spotted Cuckoo targets these birds as hosts for its chicks.

CAPE CROW ★

Swartkraai

Corvis capensis

Find Cape Crows all over the park. These noisy birds often visit picnic sites to eat the scraps of food left behind by visitors.

The Cape Crow is a shiny, all-black bird with a long bill. It feeds on larger insects, small vertebrates and parts of plants such as bulbs.

PIED CROW

Witborskraai

Corvus albus

This well-known crow is less common in the Kgalagadi than elsewhere. It feeds on fruit, nestlings and reptiles. This is the larger of the two species and the one that can soar, made possible by its broad wings.

STARLINGS

Family: Sturnidae

Number of species: 4

Starlings are small to medium-sized birds with blue to black plumage and an iridescence (glossy) and silky structure. They are arboreal or terrestrial and omnivorous, foraging mainly on the ground where they can hop and run, but they also glean from vegetation and hawk from a perch. The lateral placement of the eyes towards the front of the face enables them some binocular vision. They are monogamous and territorial but gregarious when not breeding and make seasonal movements in response to conditions.

BURCHELL'S STARLING

Grootglansspreeu

Lamprotornis australis

The Cape Glossy Starling and the Burchell's Starling prefer a similar habitat to the Bulbul. Both are glossy blue and feed on fruit and insects. They forage on the ground most of the time. The Burchell's Starling has dark brown eyes and a longish tail and is one of the largest starlings.

Enrico Liebenberg

CAPE GLOSSY STARLING ★

Kleinglansspreeu

Lamprotornis nitens

▲ The Cape Starling is a widespread species often seen in the Kgalagadi along the dry riverbeds. Both species occurring here are glossy blue, but the Cape Glossy Starling has orange-yellow eyes.

They are targeted by the Great Spotted Cuckoo, a brood-parasite, to raise their young.

PALE-WINGED STARLING

Bleekvlerkspreeu

Onychognathus nabouroup

▲ Look for Pale-winged Starlings in rocky habitats. They roost and nest on ledges or in cavities in the calcareous rocks.

They move around in small flocks, foraging in trees and on the ground for fruit and insects. This species is not widespread in the Kgalagadi. It is a near-endemic species and an uncommon resident. The Great Spotted Cuckoo, a brood parasite, targets them to raise their young.

WATTLED STARLING

Lelspreeu

Creatophora cinerea

▸ Although resident, the Wattled Starlings move around (nomadic) in response to food sources such as termites, locusts and fruits. You will find them wherever food sources are available.

These birds are omnivorous and forage on the ground in flocks. They nest and roost together. The Wattled Starling is the only species that probes into grass and soil.

They are the sole Kgalagadi species with sexual dimorphism (males and females do not look alike), and males have wattles during the breeding season. Unlike other starlings, they lack the iridescence feathers typical of most starling species.

FRUIT EATERS AND NECTAR FEEDERS

In an arid environment such as the Kalahari, fully fruit-eating birds cannot survive. Those who eat fruit must supplement their diet with leaves, flowers and nectar. Nectar-feeding birds are rare in the Kalahari as there are few flowering plants with flowers suited as a source of nectar for slender-billed nectar feeders.

MOUSEBIRDS

Family: Coliidae

Number of species: 2

Mousebirds get their name from their brown-grey, mouse-like appearance. They all have distinct crests and longish graduated tails. Mousebirds are all exclusively vegetarian and have short, substantial bills with a cutting edge for cutting off vegetation. They feed on fruit, leaves, flowers and nectar. The cellulose in vegetable matter is challenging to digest and, therefore, they have bacteria and unicellular organisms in their gut to aid fermentation. To speed up this process, they tend to sunbathe early in the morning and late afternoon, exposing the skin on their tummies with their belly feathers erect to sunlight. They do this to speed up cellulose fermentation in their stomachs. They do not generally hold a territory, are often seen in groups, and occasionally make seasonal nomadic moves in response to flowering and fruiting plants.

RED-FACED MOUSEBIRD

Rooiwangmuisvoël

Urocolius indicus

▾ This mousebird is the only mousebird with a red face and bill. It is a strong flyer and usually moves around in groups from tree to tree.

WHITE-BACKED MOUSEBIRD ★

Wirkruismuisvoël

Colius colius

▴ The White-backed Mousebird is a typical bird of the arid savanna. It may be seen hanging upside down from branches rather than perching upright. It is the smallest species and a weak flyer. It can be seen sunning its belly in the early mornings or cold days. It is endemic to southern Africa.

BARBETS

Family: Lybiidae

Number of species: 1

Barbets are medium-to-small birds with large, heavy bills that are medium in length, toothed, serrated and pointed at the tip. They nest in holes in trees excavated by themselves.

ACACIA PIED BARBET ★

Bonthoutkapper

Tricholaema leucomelas

▾ The Acacia Pied Barbet is often heard rather than seen. Its nasal 'pehp pehp pehp phe phep' call is loud and carries far. It calls all day long, from a high perch. It is usually solitary but in pairs during the breeding season. When seen in flight, it flies with a slight dipping motion. It prefers fruit, seeds and nectar.

It is a rather plump bird with a red forehead, yellow eyebrows, a black bib and striped wings. They prefer fruit, seeds and nectar (which they get from the flowers of the parasitic mistletoe).

LOVEBIRDS

Family: Psittaculidae

Number of species: 1

Birds in this family all have short, stout, deep bills hooked downwards on the upper jaw and upwards on the lower jaw. Their heads are large with short necks, stout legs and strong feet, with the middle two toes pointing forwards and the outer two facing backwards.

ROSY-FACED LOVEBIRD

Rooiwangparkiet

Agapornis roseicollis

▾ Rosy-faced Lovebirds are uncommon in the Kgalagadi but good sightings have been recorded in the northern parts of the park and along the Auob riverbed. They occur in pairs or flocks.

RO

SUNBIRDS

Family: Nectariinidae

Number of species: 2

All sunbirds have long, slender, downward-curved bills and long tongues to help them reach the nectar in flowers. In the Kgalagadi, they largely depend on the parasitic mistletoe flowers for nectar. They rely on sugar-rich nectar for energy but feed their young with insects and spiders. They also use spider webs to construct their nests.

DUSKY SUNBIRD

Namakwasuikerbekkie

Cinnyris fuscus

The Dusky Sunbird is highly active and a typical occupant of the Kgalagadi. Look for these birds on flowering shrubs or trees with mistletoe.

It is not as brightly coloured as most other sunbirds; breeding males appear black with a white belly but the black feathers have a purple, green and coppery gloss when seen in good light. The female is light grey-brown above and off-white below.

MARICO SUNBIRD

Maricosuikerbekkie

Cinnyris mariquensis

The broad maroon breastband easily identifies the males of these sunbirds. The grey females are streaked with pale yellow below. There is no distinction between breeding and non-breeding plumage.

Look for them in the thorn tree savanna. Males are pretty cheeky, giving chase when other males are in the area.

Rudolph Oosthuizen

SMALLER TERRESTRIAL BIRDS IN OPEN AREAS

Smaller terrestrial birds include all the lark species, which are almost exclusively terrestrial and feed and nest on the ground. Their diet consists of invertebrates and seeds. Some dig for food, others associate with feeding mammals that disturb insects when grazing, and the primarily short-clawed feed on insects. Several lark species are well known for tolerating extremes in temperature. These larks are not dependent on water and can survive in arid areas by including more insects in their diet, especially when they need moisture for cooling during high temperatures. Some species overcome extreme temperatures by sheltering in rodent burrows. Others seek shade and pant with their bills open to cool off by moisture evaporating from their mouths (birds have no sweat glands).

LARKS

Family: Alaudidae

Number of species: 10

The red Kalahari sand is the favoured habitat of several species of larks whose coloration perfectly matches the environment. After good rains, up to 10 species of larks might be present, but only four species are sedentary. These are the Fawn-coloured Lark, the Sabota Lark, the Spike-heeled Lark, and the Eastern Clapper Lark.

Larks are generally territorial all year round and usually have only one long-term breeding partner (monogamous). They nest on the ground and position the nest near a disruptive object such as a rock or a tuft of grass. Others may nest in the open and place a ring of pebbles around the nest, possibly acting as camouflage. This behaviour is to minimise predation because smaller predators investigate grass tussocks and rocks for food. The eggs are well camouflaged and the clutch usually hatches simultaneously. The down of many nestlings resembles the yellowish grass used for lining the nest, while the eggshells and faecal sacks are removed not to disclose the position of the nest and nestlings. In hot weather, the adults shade the nestlings and feed them on only insects. They perform clever distraction displays when a predator is approaching.

FAWN-COLOURED LARK ★

Vaalbruinlewerik

Calendulauda africanoides

Look out for Fawn-coloured Larks on the dune roads. Notice the white and broad eyebrow and white under the bill, while there is no dark line from the bill to the ear. There is a rufous panel in wing primaries, with pinkish legs.

This lark is a common resident. It is a regular sighting as it often perches on a low lookout in a horizontal position while singing. It has a wide distribution but the population in the dry western region is paler in colour. With its cryptic plumage, it is found almost exclusively on the Kalahari sands. It forages on the ground and nearly half its diet consists of grass seeds.

SABOTA LARK

Sabotalewerik

Calendulauda sabota

▲ Look out for the Sabota Larks, where stands of three-thorns or black-thorns are next to the road, mainly in the north, where the woodland is more pronounced.

The Sabota Lark is common in arid savannas and open woodlands. It has bold facial markings and a streaked back. It is highly vocal in summer and perches upright on trees and bushes when singing. It mimics a variety of other bird species in its song. Seeds make up 60% of its diet and it is not known to drink water. Note the distinct white eyebrow and streaking on the chest.

Look for the white eyebrow that stretches from the back of the head to the base of the bill. The chest is speckled dark brown, the belly is white, and it has a thin black eye stripe.

SPIKE-HEELED LARK ★

Vlaktelewerik

Chersomanes albofasciata

Look out for the white chin and tip of the relatively short tail, the long, straight hind claw from which its specific name is derived and conspicuous when sitting on a small bush or rock. Look for them on the dune roads and the bare ground surrounding pans.

The sub-species occurring in the Kgalagadi are paler in colour than elsewhere.

Spike-heeled Larks have long, down-curved bills and are familiar residents that seldom perch and can be seen in pairs or small groups foraging uprightly. When they fly, they move with a bobbing movement and a fanned tail. Insects are their primary food item but they also eat seeds. It is rare in larks that both males and females build the nests and have helpers to rear the young (cooperative breeders).

EASTERN CLAPPER LARK

Hoëveldklappertjie

Mirafra fasciolata

▼ This lark is noticed only if it performs its display flight of noisy wingbeats to show its fitness. This display consists of a steep upward flight with a clear wing rattle or clapping at the top, followed by cruising for a few minutes and clapping every 15–30 seconds on fluttering wings before it parachutes to the ground accompanied by a clear 'peeeeuu' whistle.

This species lives in the grasslands on the dunes and is a common resident. It searches the base of grass tufts for grass seeds and insects. It usually displays after rain and breeds during summer to late summer. It builds a domed nest of grass, with an entrance at the side and positions it close to a grass tuft or forb for protection and some shade.

RO

GREY-BACKED SPARROWLARK ★

Grysruglewerik

Eremopterix verticalis

▲ Grey-backed Sparrow-Larks are familiar residents. It's black underparts and large white ear patches indicate the male. The female is brownish-grey with a black patch on the centre of the belly. They have stout, conical bills indicating that they mainly feed on seeds. As seed-eaters, they drink regularly and visit water in small flocks.

STARK'S LARK

Woestynlewerik

Calandrella cinerea

These occur mainly in the south.

RED-CAPPED LARK

Rooikoplewerik

Calandrella cinerea

A small population can occur in the north towards Botswana.

MONOTONOUS LARK

Bosveldlewerik

Mirafra passerina

▲ It may occur as a vagrant but is not a true resident.

KAROO LONG-BILLED LARK

Karoolangbeklewerik

Certhilauda subcoronata

It may occur in the south but is not plentiful.

PINK-BILLED LARK

South and Nossob

Pienkbeklewerik

Spizocorys conirostriso

A small population occurs south of Nossob. Some larks are occasional nomads, including the Monotonous Lark, Red-capped Lark, Pink-billed Lark, and Stark's Lark.

SEEDEATERS WITH SOFT BILLS

Seed-eating birds such as doves, pigeons and sandgrouses do not have the seed-cracking bills of other seed-eaters and they swallow whole seeds. To assist digestion, they ingest small stones.

DOVES AND PIGEONS

Family: Columbidae
Number of species: 6

Doves are common in semi-arid environments worldwide, provided there is drinking water. In the Kgalagadi, vast flocks of Cape Turtle Doves and Laughing Doves gather in the mornings and late afternoons to drink at the artificial boreholes spread along the dry riverbeds. The daintier Namakwa Dove, with its extra-long pointed tail, is another typical sighting in semi-arid areas.

In a way, doves are similar in build to sandgrouse and feed on seeds picked up on the ground. Most families have thin, slender, soft bills and prefer whole seeds. They do, however, roost and nest in trees. As seedeaters, they must drink regularly and can survive in arid areas only where surface water is available. Doves are strong flyers that can forage far from water but cannot beat sandgrouse. When drinking, doves suck up the water and swallow without tilting their heads backwards. Doves walk rather than hop when looking for seeds on the ground but they can perch because of a well-developed hind toe.

They roost alone when breeding and are monogamous (have only one partner). The nest is a flimsy structure in trees or shrubs, strengthened by faecal waste throughout incubation and brooding. Both parents are involved in incubation and can rear several broods during their breeding. It is yet another reason why they are successful in arid environments.

Doves and pigeons are unique in feeding their chicks with a protein-rich secretion from the crop. This substance is often called pigeon milk and is the liquid secreted from the lining of the dove's crop by both the male and female. This is all the nestling needs until later, when insects and seeds supplement it.

CAPE TURTLE DOVE ★

Gewone Tortelduif
Streptopelia capicola

Cape Turtle Doves are abundant in the Kgalagadi and are regular visitors to waterholes.

As a safety measure, they congregate in huge numbers on trees close to waterholes before going down in a flock to drink. They drink at least once or twice a day and spend a relatively short time at the water; a tactic to minimise predation from opportunistic predators such as falcons, black-backed jackals, African wild cats and even herons that wait at the water until the doves fly

down in great numbers to drink before they strike and kill.

Their nests are flimsy platforms of twigs and two eggs are laid. The parents feed the chicks with a milk-like substance produced in their crops. Their loud 'kuk-koor-ko' calls can be heard throughout the day and sometimes at night.

LAUGHING DOVE ★

Rooiborsduifie

Spilopelia senegalensis

▲ Although widespread, Laughing Doves are not as numerous as Cape Turtle Doves in the Kgalagadi and are often seen foraging in the rest camps.

Laughing Doves are closely related to Cape Turtle Doves and share many features. One distinguishing characteristic is the speckling on the upper breast and the lack of a black neck collar. When they call, they typically inflate their throats. They lay up to four eggs at a time in their flimsy nests. Like the Turtle Doves, both sexes share the incubation duties; the male takes the day shift while the female incubates at night.

NAMAQUA DOVE ★

Namakwaduifie

Oena capensis

Look for these doves on the bare ground around waterholes. They are usually seen in pairs and seldom form flocks. They feed exclusively on tiny seeds but are highly nomadic during dry periods when they are scarce.

The smaller Namaqua Doves are the only ones with long, pointed tails, and males look different from females. The males have conspicuous black faces, neck fronts and orange bills. These doves prefer dry conditions but drink water daily around midday.

They breed year-round. The nest is an untidy, loose bowl of twigs in the fork of trees or on a branch, even on the ground. Two eggs hatch in a fortnight and the young are independent in another 16 days.

RED-EYED DOVE ★

Grootringduif

Streptopelia semitorquata

▼ Seldom seen and only in the far north towards Union's End.

SANDGROUSE

Family: Pteroclidae

Number of species: 3

You may hear the grouse long before you see the flock circling above as they descend to settle a few metres from the water's edge; however, you must be there at their favourite drinking place from about two hours after sunrise to experience the awe-inspiring sandgrouse spectacle. You first see the individuals properly as they march towards the waters' edge, where they spend a surprisingly short time drinking because of the danger of being caught by raptors, jackals and other predators. Within a few seconds, they are gone. Wave after wave, the flocks will arrive and take off after drinking for a mere few seconds.

Sandgrouses are a family of entirely ground-living birds adapted to survive in arid areas. Their bodies are perfectly camouflaged with plumage resembling the desert's shades. With their short legs, they move low to the ground and flick gravel aside with their short bills to select only protein-rich, relatively nutritious seeds low in toxicity, such as those of the legume family. They are generally gregarious and flocks move about to exploit temporary pockets of suitable food.

When these birds breed, they separate into monogamous pairs. The nests are superficial scrapes in the earth scantily lined with dry plant material. The eggs are specially adapted by being small with thick shells to reduce moisture loss. The female incubates two or three eggs by day, where she is exposed to the sun's direct rays for most of the time but has a longer time at feeding, while the male takes over at dusk and incubates during the night until past dawn.

The chicks are precocious, which means they hatch out in an advanced state with their eyes open and legs and feet ready for immediate locomotion. During the first weeks, they are still covered in down feathers for camouflage protection and to keep warm, and both parents still attend to them.

Sandgrouses are most vulnerable when they drink. Predators lurk around and take their chances to get a good meal or two. They must watch out for leopards and jackals, but they fear the swift Lanner Falcons perched high on surrounding camelthorns the most. Two species regularly visit mid-morning at waterholes: the Namaqua sandgrouse and the Burchell's sandgrouse.

NAMAQUA SANDGROUSE ★

Kelkiewyn

Pterocles namaqua

Namaqua Sandgrouse are so perfectly camouflaged that they are difficult to spot at their feeding grounds despite feeding in the open. They prefer stone and gravel places and rocky terrain, such as the calcrete outcrops along the Nossob and Auob riverbanks. Their feeding places may be as far away as 60–80 km from a suitable waterhole but like most sandgrouse, they fly in, usually in the mornings, with intervals of up to five days.

♂

The male has a plain yellowish head, neck and double breast band. The female has a streaked breast. Up to 6 000 can arrive in different flocks at a suitable waterhole any morning. This is spectacular to see. The Namaqua Sandgrouse is the first to arrive, followed by the closely related Burchell's Sandgrouse about an hour later. Their characteristic nasal call 'ki-ki-keeu' or kelkiewyn (the Afrikaans name) can be heard when they approach and circle the waterhole before settling to drink. Unlike the Burchell's Sandgrouse, they land some metres away from the water and walk down to its edge.

Namaqua Sandgrouse depend on rainfall for breeding, usually in early summer, from September to November.

BURCHELL'S SANDGROUSE ★

Gevlekte Sandpatrys

Pterocles burchelli

▲ Burchell's Sandgrouse (or Spotted Sandgrouse) are endemic to the red sands of the Kgalagadi Desert.

In the park, they feed and breed in the grasslands of the dunes. They can be identified by their pinkish rufous plumage below and yellowish rufous with white spots above. The male has a grey head. They arrive about an hour after the Namaqua Sandgrouse at the water, also in huge flocks. Unlike the Namaqua Sandgrouse, they land closer to the water. Their call is also different and has a staccato 'kwok-kwok' in flight.

DOUBLE-BANDED SANDGROUSE

Dubbelbandsandpatrys

Pterocles bicinctus

The male is similar to the male of the Namaqua Sandgrouse but has a black and white band across the forehead. Unlike the other two species, it drinks at sunset, is less active during the day and may be seen resting cryptically in the shadows of scrubby vegetation. It has only a small distribution in the southeast of the park.

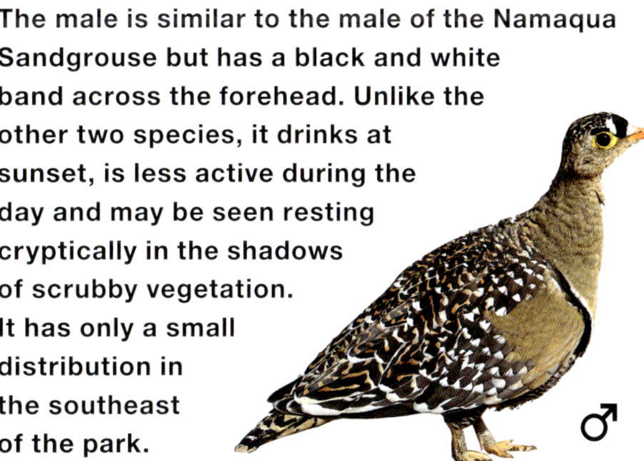

WEAVERS, QUELEAS AND SPARROWS

Family: Ploceidae

Number of species: 10

The fascination with weavers is understandable since their lifestyle and nest-building capabilities are so captivating. The weaver family is vast with approximately 120 species. Most species are associated with water and therefore only a few occur in the arid savanna. The Sociable Weaver is an icon of this thirst-land, as are the White-browed Sparrow Weaver and Scaly-feathered Weaver. Some sparrows found here have a wide distribution and can tolerate the adverse conditions of a semi-desert. These species apply relatively simple nest-building techniques using dry grass. They build nests out of grass stalks that are not woven but stuck into the nest structure. These weavers are associated with their nests throughout the year, thus maintaining the structures with periodic building in all seasons. Both sexes participate to some degree.

The true weavers weave closed nests with entrances either at the side or below. Nest-building is seasonal in the true weavers and these short-lived structures mostly do not survive beyond one breeding season. Only one species, the Southern Masked Weaver, of the true weavers (those that weave and knot) is a permanent resident. At the same time, the Red-billed Quelea is a typical nomad that is a regular but unseasonal visitor when conditions are favourable.

SOCIABLE WEAVERS ★

Versamelvoël

Philetairus socius

Driving through the Northern Cape or Namibia towards the Kgalagadi Transfrontier Park, you may notice the enormous straw masses on telephone poles, windmills and camelthorn trees. These are the homes of some of the endemic and most characteristic of all birds of the arid savanna – the Sociable Weavers. They are unobtrusive little fellows but have the most exciting lifestyle and adaptations that enable them to survive, despite the extreme nature of the land they call home.

The Sociable Weavers have adopted a colonial lifestyle. A small bird on its own Is vulnerable but there is safety in numbers, and therefore family groups live together in what can be compared to an apartment block with many small apartments.

Sociable Weavers must be superb natural architects building these massive interlocking nest chambers out of straw. For this they use different materials for various parts of the nest. They carefully select each material for its purpose. Large twigs and stems are placed at an angle and point downwards for the roof of the nest. Grasses are then shoved into the structure until it is firmly secured. Dune reed, the perennial grass that grows on the dune crests, is used for several purposes. Spikey grass stalks are arranged at the entrance of each nest to deter predators.

Such a nest mass may contain over 100 chambers and weigh 1 000 kilograms. Photographic evidence shows that nests can remain active for at least 100 years. However, in years of plentiful rain, nest masses become waterlogged and so heavy that they fall or break apart. The nest mass is usually home to about 300 paired birds.

Insects and seeds (primarily green grasses) compose nearly their entire diet. Since insects make up 80 percent of their primary food supplement, they obtain most of their moisture from this but they also drink water if it is available. Harvester termites are the most important source of food.

Snakes, especially Cape cobras, are common nest predators. They often consume all the eggs in all the chambers of a large nest and nest predation is high; in one study, 70 percent of the clutches laid were predated.

A pair of Pygmy Falcons usually takes over one or two chambers in the nest mass: one for breeding and one for roosting. The weavers tolerate this intruder, although Pygmy Falcons have been known to help themselves to one or more of the chicks. They mostly prefer the skinks that are commonly found on camelthorns.

Other birds the weavers tolerate are the Yellow-billed Hornbill, Lilac-breasted Roller, Grey-headed Sparrow and others. Unwelcome intruders include the Acacia Pied Barbet and aerial and canopy predators such as the Chanting and Gabar Goshawks. Honey badgers and yellow mongooses also pose a threat.

Nest colonies don't only house weavers, but they are also a hotspot for a lot of activity and biodiversity. Several hangers-on choose to live in, under or on these nest masses. More skinks are found on trees with these nest masses than on others. Cheetahs are known to climb to the top of such colonies to use the roof as a vantage point. The African pygmy falcon relies solely on Sociable Weaver nest chambers for breeding and large birds such as Spotted Eagle-Owls, vultures and snake eagles often use the platforms created by these structures as a safe refuge or for nesting. Tree-climbing mammals include wild cats, mongooses and genets. Other bird species that regularly take advantage of the nest cavities for roosting or breeding are Acacia Pied Barbets, Ashy Tits, Scaly-feathered Finches and even Barn Owls that make use of inner cavities for nesting.

Recent research findings show weaver colonies are essential in the arid savanna. Their role will become even more important as climate changes advance, especially for species that use them as refuges against harsh ambient temperatures.

If you come across one of these colonies next to the road, park your vehicle and look and listen. The constant chatter of the birds and the abundant energy and liveliness of a colony are truly mesmerising.

SOUTHERN MASKED WEAVER ★

Swartkeel Geelvink

Ploceus velatus

The Southern Masked Weaver is recognisable by its red eyes and yellow crown.

When breeding, the male wears a black mask from the forecrown to the face and throat, ending in a point; the crown, neck and underparts are yellow, the bill is black and the upperparts are greenish-yellow. The non-breeding plumage is brownish-green above, while the throat is cream, the breast pale buff and the belly white.

RED-BILLED BUFFALO WEAVER

Buffelwewer

Bubalornis niger

Red-billed Buffalo Weavers are uncommon on the South African side of the Kgalagadi and occur more on the Botswana side.

Buffalo Weavers, White-browed Sparrow-weavers and Sociable Weavers are closely allied. All three of these species tend to stay in their nests throughout the year and, by doing this, they save energy and require less food. Buffalo Weavers are the only weavers with black plumage. The sexes do not look alike – the adult male is black except for a white wing bar, conspicuous in flight, and the red bill. Adult females are dark-brown in the upperparts, tail, throat, chest and belly, while the under tail is mottled with white and has a red bill.

RED-BILLED QUELEA

Rooibekkwelea

Quelea quelea

Red-billed Queleas are typical nomadic seedeaters that follow rainfall for an abundant food supply.

These are small weavers with short tails and wings and compact conical bills. The males have distinct breeding and non-breeding plumage and the bill colour may change seasonally for both sexes. They are gregarious and feed, drink and roost together.

SCALY-FEATHERED FINCH (WEAVER) ★

Baardmannetjie

Sporopipes squamifrons

Look out for flocks of tiny Scaly-feathered Finches as you drive along areas further away from the dry riverbeds. They are abundant on the dunes as you drive towards the Auchterlonie historic site and picnic area or along the Nossob River road northwards after the Melkvlei Picnic Site, where black-thorn acacias are abundant. Of course, they are found all over the park but if you have yet to come across them, you will find them where there isn't much else.

These finches are a remarkable desert-adapted bird species. They are social birds and live in flocks of about 20 individuals. You will probably find them busily moving around and foraging on the ground in their group. As you get closer, the whole flock will retreat with a whirring sound to a nearby small thorn bush. This behaviour will enable you to look at them properly with your binoculars as they are tiny birds.

Their most distinctive features are their black-and-white malar stripes, which resemble a moustache. The sexes look alike and have an overall whitish to light-grey unobtrusive colouring. Their bills, however, are a pretty light pink. Those with horn-coloured bills and inconspicuous malar stripes will be juveniles.

Look out for their nests in thorn bushes along the way, especially where black-thorns or young camelthorns grow close to the road. From far away, the nest resembles an untidy clump of dry grass stuck to the thinner outer branches of a thorny bush. There usually is only one of these messy, rugby-ball-shaped nests per shrub. They do not weave the grasses like other weavers, but bend them when constructing the nest. Nests are used for roosting and breeding and are one to four metres above the ground.

WHITE-BROWED SPARROW-WEAVERS ★

Koringvoël

Plocepasser mahali

White-browed Sparrow-weavers are plentiful in the park. Look for their nests on the southwestern side of camelthorns. They have a much wider distribution than Sociable Weavers and are increasingly extending their range south and eastwards as rising temperatures affect the environment. They are particularly successful when conditions are hot and dry but are also vulnerable to increasing temperatures since their lifestyle has given them some advantages.

Recognise these birds by their brown and white colour, the prominent white eyebrow, and the big white rump. Males have black beaks, females have horn-coloured beaks and juveniles have pinkish-brown beaks.

Food consists largely of insects, especially harvester termites and seeds. Insects provide sufficient moisture for adults and chicks, although the birds will drink when water is available. The birds often forage on the ground in groups, which may also be for safety in numbers.

They engage in cooperative breeding and the helpers assist the breeding pair in defending the territory around the nesting sites. The dominant male's vocalisation plays a vital role in fending off unwanted intruders of the same species that seek a challenge.

From first light, the dominant male sings his long, rambling song from the entrance to his roosting nest and later from perches within his territory. Other males may reply with their song. Sometimes, the helpers join a group song chorus, especially if an intruder is spotted.

The main predators of Sparrow-weavers are falcons and kites and little can be done when an aerial attack is imminent. Making a din seldom works. On the other hand, snakes sneak up and quickly raid the breeding nests of eggs and chicks. The semi-desert environment houses many reptiles and snakes and the Cape cobra is one of the biggest threats. The nest-raiding African Harrier-Hawk also poses a problem for nestlings.

♀

SPARROWS

Family: Passeridae

Number of species: 4

Birds of this family are reasonably small passerines with short- to medium-length conical bills. Their plumages are primarily brown, with yellow in some species and do not show seasonal changes. In some cases, the colour of the bill changes during breeding.

CAPE SPARROW ★

Gewone Mossie

Passer melanurus

Look out for Cape Sparrows in and around camps where they forage on the ground, hopping from one spot to the next.

The Cape Sparrow is a striking, un-streaked, brightly coloured sparrow with different-looking males and females. The male has a distinctive bold, black head and throat with a striking white crescent extending from the eye around the ear. The female has a pale grey head with a buff or pale crescent, similar in shape to the male's. A prominent white wing bar and white underparts are distinguishing features.

Pairs and small flocks are resident in various natural and human-altered habitats. House Sparrows have streaked backs and lack the distinctive facial pattern of the Cape Sparrow. It is a sociable species and often mixes with House Sparrows, but during breeding time it usually groups together in family groups or pairs.

The bird's natural habitat is open grassland and scrubby vegetation, where it feeds on grass seeds, fresh blossoms and insects. Like all seed-eating birds, it needst needs to drink regularly and arrives in big numbers at the waterholes, where it joins other seedeaters for a drink.

Most interesting is that this species is near-endemic, with only a fractional population in southwestern Angola. This resident is common and abundant and well adapted to the harsh environment of the Kgalagadi. Unlike the imported alien House Sparrows, they build their nests in thorny trees. The nests are large, untidy, ball-shaped structures with a side entrance. Instead of lining the nest with feathers, they prefer fresh sprigs of aromatic herbs. The reason for this needs to be investigated but it is a fascinating subject for debate while game viewing. The nest provides enough insulation for significant energy savings, paramount in an environment with extreme temperatures.

Another interesting fact is that this sparrow species, indigenous and widely available, has become a target species for the Diederik Cuckoo, a brood parasite, to raise its young.

GREAT SPARROW

Grootmossie

Passer motitensis

The adult male is larger than the similar-looking House Sparrow. Notice the short, thick bill and small, black bib. The very short white eyebrow is diagnostic. The female has no bib nor rufous rump, but a creamy broad eyebrow. Notice the heavy bill and pale cheeks.

HOUSE SPARROW

Huismossie

Passer domesticus

The male has a grey crown and nape, a black bib and pink legs and feet. The female is grey-brown above and whitish below. The crown is grey, the eyebrows are white and the eye stripe is dark grey.

SOUTHERN GREY-HEADED SPARROW ★

Gryskopmossie

Passer diffuses

▾ This medium-sized, slim sparrow has a plain grey head and a single white wing stripe. The sexes are alike.

ESTRILDID FINCHES (WAXBILLS)

Family: Estrildidae

Number of species: 5

Several small granivorous birds are colloquially referred to as finches, even if they don't belong to the same family. The Red-headed Finch and Cut-throat Finch are the true finches, but only the former occurs in the Kgalagadi. Waxbills are regular seasonal visitors to the Kgalagadi. Their conical bills are ideal for cracking and dehusking grass seeds before swallowing them. They prefer habitats with substantial grass cover for the seeds but supplement their diet with insects.

Only two of the nine southern African species are common in the Kgalagadi. These tiny finches have striking plumage and soft, simple songs. Gregarious and often colonial, most estrildids huddle together when roosting, and you will frequently see them preening their partners. They usually build large domed grass nests but viduine finches parasitize the nests of most species. The Shaft-tailed Whydah targets the Violet-eared Waxbill as a host for rearing its offspring. The Black-faced Waxbill, which is less common, may also occasionally serve as a host for this brood parasite.

The best place to find and watch finches and waxbills is at a pool of water. They are numerous at Dalkeith and Craigh Lochardt in the Auob riverbed, as well as many other water troughs that have an overflow.

RED-HEADED FINCH ★

Rooikopvink

Amadina erythrocephala

▾ These are true finches and widespread in the Kgalagadi.

They feed on both seeds and insects, are gregarious and flocks may number several hundred. They are prone to nomadism. Compared to the waxbills, they are large, heavy-billed birds and more like sparrows.

♀

♂

BLACK-FACED WAXBILL ★

Swartwangsysie

Estrilda erythronotos

▴ The adults have black faces, barred wings and bright-red rumps. Sexes are alike but females are paler. Black-faced Waxbills occur in pairs or groups of their kind, or they join other seedeaters. They feed on grass, inflorescences or seeds on the ground.

VIOLET-EARED WAXBILL ★

Koningblousysie

Uraeginthus granatinus

These species are common residents but are nomadic in the dry season.

The Violet-eared Waxbill is one of the breathtaking tiny beauties of the arid savanna. As a seedeater, it drinks regularly when water is available and seems less nomadic than other seedeaters, which follow the rains to share in the abundance of seeds after new growth. They may supplement their diet with insects such as termites.

Waxbills are monogamous with biparental care and the males look different from the females. The birds usually arrive in pairs at the water, except in late summer when juveniles may accompany them. They breed from December to May and their nests are roughly constructed balls of grass with a side entrance placed in a thorny bush. Both males and females build nests, with the male often bringing nesting material to the female.

Violet-eared Waxbills are the primary hosts of the brood parasitic Shaft-tailed Whydah. The whydahs learn their hosts' songs, which they use during their courtship displays.

Because of their tiny size, Violet-eared Waxbills are particularly vulnerable to overheating. Behavioural adaptations cushion the effect of extreme temperature by huddling together and roosting in deep shade.

RED-BILLED FIREFINCH

Rooibekvuurvinkie

Lagonosticta senegala

▲ The beautiful Red-billed Firefinch is uncommon in the Kgalagadi, but occurs in the extreme south.

Males and females differ in plumage, with the male having a red throat and belly, small white spots on flanks, brown upperparts and a red bill. The female has a small red patch on her forehead, a sandy-brown head, brown upperparts, small white spots on her chest and a pinkish bill.

GREEN-WINGED PYTILIA

Gewone Melba

Pytilia melba

The Green-winged Pytilia occurs in the Kgalagadi but is also a seasonal visitor.

WHYDAHS

Family: Viduidae

Number of species: 1

The whydahs and their allies are small- to medium-sized birds with short conical bills adapted for seed eating. The entire family are brood parasites and all but one species paratisizing estrildid finches (waxbills). Brood parasites are birds that rely on others to raise their young. The brood parasite manipulates a host to raise its young as if it were its own, using different kinds of mimicry such as mouth markings of the chicks that resemble the host.

Only one species occurs in the Kgalagadi. Male whydahs court their mates with exaggerated tail plumes and postures.

SHAFT-TAILED WHYDAH ★

Pylstertrooibekkie

Vidua regia

The Shaft-tailed Whydah occurs only in southern Africa, from South Africa to Angola. These birds prefer open and drier areas such as those found in arid savanna, and they feed exclusively on grass seeds, which they look for on the ground. It uses the technique of scratching up buried seeds, which pre-adapts it for life in the arid sector of southern Africa. Being granivorous, it drinks water when available but can go without for long periods.

During the non-breeding season, the male and female Shaft-tailed Whydah are unobtrusive small birds with reddish-orange bills and legs, streaky upperparts and pale buffy underparts. However, everything changes in summer, during breeding season, when the male transforms from drab to a stunning guise; whereas the female retains her muted brownish plumage. The breeding male has buffy-orange underparts and neck, a dark cap and 17-centimetre black tail feathers. Breeding males hold territories in dry thorn scrub but form flocks with other seedeaters after breeding.

The Shaft-tailed Whydah is polygynous, with the male having several females in his group. The jerky flight display of the breeding male is distinctive. When singing or calling, he does so from a high calling site and will mimic the call of the Violet-eared Waxbill. He will also defend his territory from neighbouring males that may be less than 100 metres from him. It is interesting to note that females are particular about their suitors. Tail length plays a vital role in the success of a male. When a female enters his territory, he hovers above her for several minutes, jerking his tail or perching nearby with fluttering wings.

The Shaft-tailed Whydah is a brood parasite on waxbills. The Violet-eared Waxbill is the primary host, although it sometimes uses the Black-faced Waxbill. Breeding females monitor the activities of their waxbill host and lay eggs in the nest of the unsuspecting hosts when conditions are right. The parasite and waxbill young are often raised successfully together because there is a remarkable similarity in mouth markings between the chicks of the whydah and their waxbill host.

BUNTINGS

Family: Emberizidae

Number of species: 2

The birds in this family are small- to mid-size and have small, cone-shaped bills. Most of their diet consists of seeds but many species also eat insects. The plumage is highly variable, generally brightly coloured and sometimes drab. In some species the sexes are similar, while in others the males have more colourful plumage. Immatures are duller than adults. Only two species are residents in the Kgalagadi.

Most birds in this family are monogamous during the breeding season. Nests are usually placed in a tree, although some species make their nest on the ground or in a bush.

LARK-LIKE BUNTING

Vaalstreepkoppie

Emberiza impetuani

The Lark-like Bunting often perches on a rock or bush from where it sings. The song is a short series of varied scratchy trills but the distinctive flight call is brief, dry, crisp one-note 'tec', which betrays its presence. It tends to flock with other seedeaters, lacking the black belly patch of the otherwise similar female sparrow-larks. It forages on the ground and jumps up to reach seeds on grass seed heads.

This little dull, nondescript, slender, buffy bunting is indeed one of the so-called LBJs, which stands for 'Little Brown Job'. Subtle features include a rusty wing panel, a pale spot near the ear, a buffy eyebrow and a small, pale, silvery bill. Pairs can be low-density esidents but, typically, the species is nomadic and large flocks erupt into the semi-arid Karoo, Kalahari and Namib after rainfall events. It prefers areas with bare, stony soil and close to pools of drinking water.

They only have one partner when breeding and their nest is a shallow cup of grass and twigs lined with fine grass placed on the ground. Snakes and small carnivores are their primary predators and nesting success is often meagre.

GOLDEN-BREASTED BUNTING

Rooirugstreepkoppie

Emberiza flaviventris

The Golden-breasted Bunting is one of the stunningly-coloured buntings with a brilliant golden breast, a yellow throat, a boldly black-and-white striped head, a chestnut back and white wing bars.

When flushed, it shows white outer tail feathers. The female is duller. Pairs and small flocks are residents, but they make local movements in arid savannas, where they forage on the ground and fly up into trees when flushed or singing. The species has a mellow descending two-note 'whit-wheeer' nasal call and a sweet, clearly whistled 'tree-chee-tree-chee' song.

CANARIES

Family: Fringillidae

Number of species: 3

This family consists of seedeaters with conical bills and notched tails. Many are nomadic, wandering in winter in search of abundant seeds. Most species flock outside the breeding season and many form flocks during the breeding season. Many canaries have undulating flight patterns and may give calls while on flight. They inhabit shrubby edges and are usually seen next to the Kgalagadi roads. Most canary species are sexually dimorphic (males look different from females) and monogamous and although the females generally incubate the eggs, both sexes help tend the young. Unlike many seed-eating birds that feed protein-rich insects to their young, many canary species feed their young mostly seeds.

YELLOW CANARY ★

Geelkanarie

Crithagra flaviventris

The Yellow Canary is widespread in the Kgalagadi and is can be spotted at Craigh Lockhart waterhole in the Auob riverbed, but is regularly seen all over the park.

This beautiful, large canary with different-looking males and females is a common near-endemic resident and local nomad in the Kgalagadi. The male has bright yellow underparts, yellow-green upperparts and a well-marked face pattern. The female is drab, grey-brown with streaky underparts, yellowish edges on the wing feathers and a yellow rump.

The Yellow Canary is more territorial than many other canary species. Pairs and small groups occupy the arid thornveld and feed on seeds, nectar, flowers and fruits while occasionally taking insects. Their melodious twittering warble can last up to half an hour.

BLACK-THROATED CANARY

Bergkanarie

Crithagra atrogularis

This canary has a bright yellow rump and white-tipped tail that is visible in flight. It is mainly resident and sedentary, although it may wander short distances in the dry season in search of water. It feeds primarily on seeds, flowers, nectar and insects such as aphids and harvester termites, doing most of its foraging on the ground and in the foliage of shrubs, forbs and small trees.

WHITE-THROATED CANARY

Witkeelkanarie

Crithagra albogularis

White-throated canaries only occur in the far north and far south of the park.

BIRDS FEEDING IN AND AROUND WATER

Waterbirds are only adapted to live with permanent water and residents are scarce. Surprisingly, several have eked out their existence in the Kgalagadi and are considered residents.

HERONS

Family: Ardeidae

Number of species: 3

Herons come in all shapes and sizes and most species are water associated. The arid Kgalagadi is not a suitable habitat for herons and it is only in wet years that some species visit to utilise the temporary presence of aquatic prey, insects and birds gathering at the water to drink.

BLACK-HEADED HERON

Swartkopreier

Ardea melanocephala

Look for these birds in the veld near the water. Several individuals have kept close to waterholes, such as Vaalpan.

Like the Grey Heron, the Black-headed Heron is a vagrant visiting this arid region during good years. It usually forages in open veld but as a great opportunist, it has learnt to wait at waterholes to catch birds coming to drink.

GREY HERON

Bloureier

Ardea cinerea

Look for the Grey Heron on the ground or in surrounding trees in open areas close to waterholes. A pair used to reside at Leeudril waterhole, catching amphibians and birds that came to drink.

Grey Herons are primarily fish eaters. However, in this arid region, they have adapted to catch other prey species such as frogs (platannas), reptiles, insects and even birds coming to the water to drink. They adopt a wait-and-strike strategy or hunt by slowly walking forward and surprising the prey.

Enrico Liebenberg

WESTERN CATTLE EGRET

Veereier

Bubulcus ibis

Look for cattle egrets in the mid-eastern section of the park with standing water in pans or at waterholes. They are not directly dependent on water but drink regularly and usually roost on vegetation near water.

During exceptional wet years, some other species in this family, such as bitterns and egrets, may surprise visitors. Cattle egrets are not common in dry areas and, therefore, in the Kgalagadi, but because they feed on grasshoppers and other insects, they often follow the game to feast on insects disturbed by grazers.

HAMERKOP

Family: Scopidae

Number of species: 1

This unique bird is typical at inland water bodies such as small temporary pools after abundant rains.

HAMERKOP

Hamerkop

Scopus umbretta

The Hamerkop is not a common resident of the Kgalagadi but occurs in the Botswana section to the northeast.

This big, dark-brown bird with a prominent crest at the back of its head may occasionally be seen at the waterholes fishing for invertebrates and frogs.

DUCKS AND GEESE

Family: Anatidae

Number of species: 4

Waterfowl species such as ducks and geese play a crucial role in the park's ecosystem, often congregating at waterholes and seasonal pans. Ducks can be spotted dabbling in the water, while geese species like the Egyptian Goose may be seen grazing on the surrounding grasslands. Despite the arid conditions of the park, the presence of water sources sustains these avian inhabitants, providing essential habitat and resources.

EGYPTIAN GOOSE

Kolgans

Alopochen aegyptiaca

The Egyptian Goose is nomadic in response to conditions. Usually associated with open water bodies, the Kgalagadi does not offer ideal habitats for them.

Yet, it is a highly adaptable bird, perhaps because it is mainly a grazer and grass-seed stripper but it will also take insects and other animal matter. They are noisy lookalike birds; only differing in their call. The male utters a 'ha-ha' and the female answers with a 'honk-honk'.

RED-BILLED TEAL

Rooibekeend

Anas erythrorhyncha

Red-billed Teals are another nomadic species that can be spotted after plentiful rains in the Kgalagadi.

They are vegetarians but also take invertebrates. You can recognise them by their red bill, dark-brown crown and pale cheeks.

SOUTH AFRICAN SHELDUCK

Kopereend

Tadorna cana

The Shelduck is well adapted to semi-dry areas such as the Kgalagadi but its preferred habitat is shallow wetlands.

It is intermittently seen when pans have water.

CAPE TEAL

Teeleend

Anas capensis

It is a nomadic species that prefers salt pans and brackish wetlands with emergent vegetation such as those in the Kgalagadi.

GREBES

Family: PODICIPEDIDAE

Number of species: 1

These small, diving birds can be observed at various waterholes and seasonal pans throughout the park, where they hunt for fish and aquatic invertebrates. Despite the park's predominantly dry environment, the presence of grebes highlights the importance of water sources in sustaining diverse ecosystems within the Kgalagadi Transfrontier Park.

LITTLE GREBE

Kleindobbertjie

Tachybaptus ruficollis

This species may occasionally be seen in the south of the park.

This is the smallest of the grebes and is not widespread in the arid savanna. It feeds on aquatic organisms, including fish, crustaceans, molluscs and amphibians. It is nomadic.

AVOCETS AND STILTS

Family: Recurvirostridae

Number of species: 2

Seldom seen, but are sometimes spotted visiting the south of the park.

BLACK-WINGED STILT

Rooipootelsie

Himantopus himantopus

Black-winged Stilts are not too particular about habitat but need a water environment. It's therefore surprising that these birds occur in the Kgalagadi, although their distribution is limited to the south, where there tends to be open water.

PIED AVOCET

Bontelsie

Recurvirostra avosetta

Pied Avocets are nomadic and occur in areas within the park similar to the stilt.

It feeds mainly on insects, small crustaceans, molluscs, worms, larvae and plant matter and prefers calm, saline water bodies.

SANDPIPERS AND GREENSHANK

Family: Scolopacidae

Number of species: 2

The sandpiper and the greenshank are common migrants but do not breed in the park.

WOOD SANDPIPER

Bosruiter

Tringa glareola

The Wood Sandpiper is a non-breeding common migrant. It feeds on aquatic organisms, including fish, crustaceans, molluscs and amphibians. It prefers shallow water and usually arrives in high summer after rains.

COMMON GREENSHANK

Groenpootruiter

Tringa nebularia'

The Common Greenshank is a summer visitor from Europe and Asia, but is seldom seen in the park.

Index

Spotted Eagle-Owl

Swallow-tailed Bee-eater

BIBLIOGRAPHY

Carlyon, John. 2011. *Nocturnal Birds of Southern Africa*. Published by author.

Carnaby, Trevor. 2008. *Beat about the Bush. Birds.* Jacana Media.

Carruthers, Vincent. 2000. *The Wildlife of Southern Africa. A Field Guide to the Animals and Plants of the Region.* Struik Publishers.

Chittenden, Hugh. 2012. *Roberts Bird Guide. A comprehensive field guide to over 950 bird species in southern Africa.* The Trustees of John Voelcker Bird Book Fund.

Cillié, Burger et al. 2022. *Birds of Southern Africa, The complete photographic guide.* Game Parks Publishing and Sunbirds Publishers.

Dennis, Nigel, Knight, Michael and Joyce, Peter.1997. *The Kalahari, Survival in a Thirstland Wilderness.* Struik Publishers.

Hockey, PAR, Dean, WRJ and PG Ryan. *Roberts Birds of Southern Africa VIIth Edition.* The Trustees of John Voelcker Bird Book Fund.

Lovegrove, Barry. 1993. *The living deserts of southern Africa. Vlaeberg, South Africa:* Fernwood Press.

Maclean, Gordon Lindsay.1993. *Roberts' birds of southern Africa. Sixth Edition, Cape Town, South Africa:* Trustees of the John Voelcker Bird Book Fund.

Mills, Gus and Margie. 2013. *A Natural History Guide to the Arid Kalahari including the Kgalagadi Transfrontier Park.* Africa Geographic Books – Black Eagle Media (Pty) Ltd.

Mills, Gus and Hes, Lex. 1997. *The Complete Book of Southern African Mammals.* Struik Winchester.

Newman, Kenneth. 1971. *Birdlife in Southern Africa.* Purnell & Sons S.A. (Pty) Ltd.

Nussey, Wilf. 1993. *The crowded desert: the Kalahari Gemsbok National Park.* Rivonia, South Africa: William Waterman.

Oberprieler, Ulrich and Cillie, Burger. 2002. *Raptor Identification Guide of Southern Africa.* Random House.

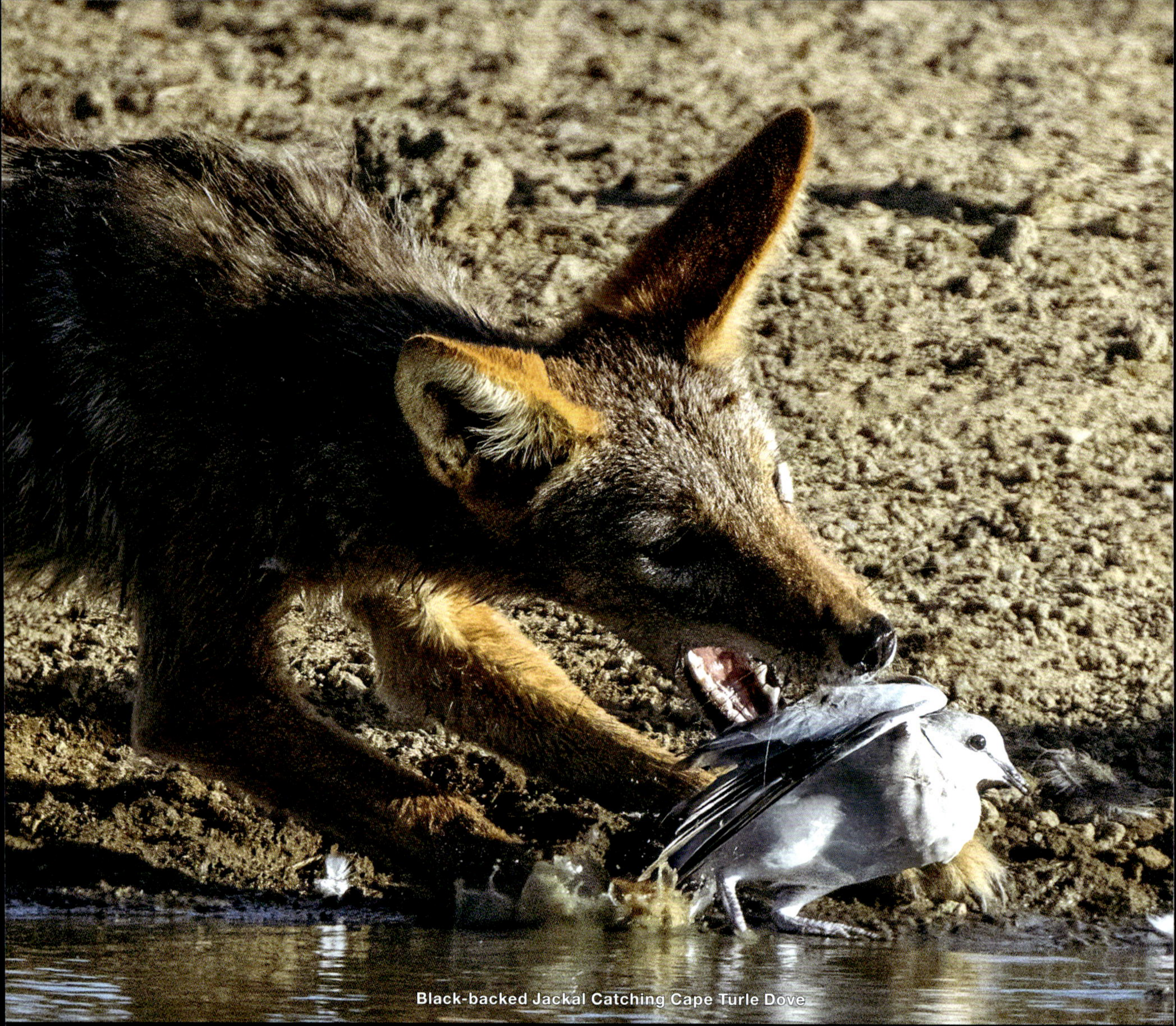

Black-backed Jackal Catching Cape Turle Dove

First Edition
ISBN 978-1-7764332-6-1
Text by Philip & Ingrid van den Berg
Photography by Philip & Ingrid van den Berg, Heinrich van den Berg
Additional photography by Enrico Liebenberg (EL), Gerda van Schalkwyk, Rudolph Oosthuizen (RO)
Publisher: Heinrich van den Berg
Edited by Jane Bowman
Proofread by Margy Gibson
Design, typesetting and reproduction by Heinrich van den Berg and Nicky Wenhold
Printed in China

First edition, first impression 2024
Published by **HPH Publishing**
50A Sixth Street, Linden, Johannesburg, 2195, South Africa
www.hphpublishing.co.za
info@hphpublishing.co.za